After early experience with J.C. Williamson's, Sydney University Dramatic Society (SUDS), Nimrod Theatre and Melbourne Theatre Company, Nick Enright trained for the theatre at New York University School of the Arts, where he studied playwriting with Israel Horovitz.

His plays include *On the Wallaby, Daylight Saving, St James Infirmary, Mongrels, A Property of the Clan, The Quartet From Rigoletto, Blackrock, Good Works, Playgrounds, Spurboard, Chasing the Dragon* and *A Poor Student*. With Justin Monjo, he adapted Tim Winton's *Cloudstreet* for the stage.

For film Nick wrote *Lorenzo's Oil* with George Miller (for which they were nominated for Academy and WGA Awards for Best Original Screenplay), and *Blackrock*; and for television *Coral Island* and the miniseries *Come In Spinner*. Many of his plays have been broadcast and he has also written original work for radio.

With composer Terence Clarke, he wrote the musicals *The Venetian Twins* and *Summer Rain*. Other musical collaborations include *Miracle City* with Max Lambert, *Mary Bryant* and *The Good Fight* with David King and the book for the Australian production of *The Boy From Oz*.

Good Works and *Cloudstreet* won Melbourne Green Room Awards for Best Play. *Daylight Saving, A Property of the Clan, Blackrock* (screenplay) and *Cloudstreet* have all won Writers' Guild Gold AWGIE Awards. Nick was honoured to receive the 1998 Sidney Myer Performing Arts Award.

Nick had long been involved as a teacher and writer with young actors, especially at the National Institute of Dramatic Art (NIDA) and the Western Australian Academy of Performing Arts (WAAPA), as well as community-based companies such as Freewheels. He was recently instrumental in setting up, with Jessica Machin and Julian Louis, State of Play, an actors' ensemble in Sydney which develops and presents new works.

Nick Enright died in Sydney in March 2003.

For George Ogilvie

ST JAMES INFIRMARY

Nick Enright

Currency Press
Sydney

CURRENCY PLAYS

First published in 1993
by Currency Press Pty Ltd,
Gadigal Land, Suite 310, 46–56 Kippax Street, Surry Hills, NSW 2010, Australia
enquiries@currency.com.au
www.currency.com.au

Reprinted in 2005, 2009, 2016

Cataloguing-in-publication data for this title is available from the National Library of Australia website: www.nla.gov.au.
Cover design by Kate Florance for Currency Press.

Currency Press acknowledges the Traditional Owners of the Country on which we live and work. We pay our respects to all Aboriginal and Torres Strait Islander Elders, past and present.

Contents

Twenty-five Years On…

George Ogilvie

The protest marches against the war in Vietnam, events which took place twenty-five years ago, represented fundamental changes in the lives of many young people in Australia. In questioning the war itself, they discovered the safety and security of their 'lucky country' depended on an unchanging world. A world which demanded adherence to conservative values and which frowned upon individualistic lifestyles.

Most disturbed by these events were the emerging artists. They found a hide-bound 'male' attitude among their peers, resulting in a brutalising effect on any creative endeavour.

The above were my stray thoughts when I first saw this play being performed by Peter Kingston. I was profoundly moved by the performance and swept back to a time when, as a young director, I was standing in court giving character references for young actors accused of protesting the arrival of the American President. A terrible but nonetheless exciting time for all of us working in the theatre.

Protest brought with it discussion and argument, and the love-hate relationship so many of us had with our own country was probed and answers sought. Having spent the previous few years studying and working in Europe, I returned to find many young minds ready for change and anxious to pull Australia out of the closeted attitudes of the fifties.

As the war escalated, the older generation also responded. I remember one night in the theatre during a performance of *The Knack* when one of the young actors, torn apart by the war news, stepped forward on stage and read out his protest. The audience heard him out in silence, and then a middle-aged member stood and said, 'Thank you young man, but you know, I think we all agree'. Thunderous applause followed, and the play continued.

Helmut Bakaitis, the Artistic Director of the Q Theatre in Penrith, was a young aspiring actor in the late sixties and was part of the change which took place in our theatre thinking. Twenty-five years later, when he read *St James Infirmary* soon after its NIDA debut, he did not hesitate to offer a production and Nick began to rework the play. Working with him will remain one of my most reassured experiences, and the chance to do a production, a high point in my career. A totally dedicated cast of fine actors brought the play with its fervour of the late sixties to wonderful life.

The characters of *St James Infirmary* stand on either side of a line. Dominic and Timothy stand on one side with their 'differences' and all the others remain entrenched on the other, upholding the only world they have known or been taught to believe in. Only Jennifer dares to cross the line, learning in the process what it's like to defy a system and become isolated in the efforts to become an individual. Brian, perhaps the saddest character in the play, will continue to live a life he now questions but which provides him with security and tradition.

Father D'Arcy is the artist who will use the system rather than defy it; a perfectly respected way of life, in the tradition of the end justifying the means. It is fascinating to think that the Church, once a bastion of conservative living, is now at the front line of protest in so many countries.

The Vietnam War became the springboard for change, and Nick Enright, himself a student at the time, with this profound play has perfectly captured the dilemma facing both young and old. A measure of its importance lies in the rehearsals of *St James*, when to my surprise I discovered that events which I took part in were, twenty-five years later, relevant to young actors rehearsing the roles. The right to question remains forbidden in many countries still and gives rise to passionate outbursts by playwrights. Nick forges a new link in this chain that surely began with Sophocles when he presented Antigone to his audience and the tradition of protest began, using the theatre as an instrument for change.

Sydney, 1992

Painting the Old School Red

Gerard Windsor

In about May 1964 I was living in seclusion outside Melbourne when I received a letter from Nick Enright. I have always remembered one phrase from it. 'Six glorious lengths', he wrote. It was his partisan race-caller's summary of the Sydney GPS Head of the River regatta that year. St Ignatius College, Riverview, the school he was still at, and that I had left eighteen months before, had won, rather convincingly. The thirteen-year-old Nick was chuffed, and so, I admit, was I.

Thrilling oarsmanship was not, however, the only stimulation to be encountered at Riverview. In *St James Infirmary* there are high grade traces of Nick Enright not just in the central artist figure, Dominic Connolly, but in all the boys portrayed or mentioned. The biographer could point out that Nick Enright was the brains of the school, that he played Hamlet (and the Scottish Lady, if not quite Lydia Languish), and that, with the encouragement of several masters, he wrote sketches for the Mavis Bramston Show.

The school had a unique, if eclectic, culture. But it also did have some hiccupping form of A Cultural Tradition. My first year as a pupil coincided with the last year of Robert Hughes and my own last coincided with Nick Enright's first. Years ago Hughes wrote for *The London Magazine* a highly entertaining and wildly inaccurate account of his Riverview schooldays, and one story has an exact counterpart in *St James Infirmary*. Hughes was caught by his Division Prefect with a copy of *The Essential James Joyce*. He wickedly defended himself with the quite truthful claim that it had been lent him by the Rector. In Nick Enright's play the book becomes the more up-to-date, and more dramatically pointed, *The Naked and the Dead*. The liberal sophisticates did in fact exist. Fitfully some Jesuits took pride in Hopkins and Robert Southwell being of their number, and I recall, as a boy of fourteen, being given to learn and recite for a meeting of the Third Division Boarders' Debating Society, *Campion's Brag*, as fine a piece as any of Elizabethan prose.

Robert Southwell lurks as one of my three discernible ingredients for the figure of the school's patron, St James Northcott—the others being St Ignatius Loyola and Sir John Northcott, the ex-army governor of NSW for most of the 1950s. For the GPS element in the school—competitively sporty, ambitious for social standing, biased towards the conservative side of politics, British as well as Australian—constituted as much of the ethos of the school as did the Jesuit tradition. In fact the two could saunter along very harmoniously together. Nick Enright's sole Jesuit character, the artistic, Machiavellianly pastoral Fr D'Arcy, inevitably brings to my mind the high-profile Fr Martin D'Arcy, boss of Campion Hall, the Jesuit residence at Oxford, and chaplain-in-chief to Evelyn Waugh, Edith Sitwell et al. Years ago I was taught a clerihew about him by the composer Malcolm Williamson, one of the last of that long line of eccentric artist converts to Catholicism.

> *Are you rich and nobly born?*
> *Is your soul in torment torn?*
> *Come and I will heal it all,*
> *Father D'Arcy, Campion Hall.*

More fundamentally, however, I think that some of the classic, often-hoped-for, rarely-realised results of Jesuit education underlie *St James Infirmary*. It is strikingly a morality play. One of its more modern begetters is the Tempters' sequence in Eliot's *Murder in the Cathedral*. Far beyond that, however, the play is a version of Christ in the desert, weak and vulnerable after his fasting, being tempted by Satan. Dominic Connolly, in his sickbed, doubly isolated by being on an island (Riverview is on a peninsular), and then in the infirmary, is tempted with community esteem and family comfort and money and the capitals of the world and lap-dog devotion if he will submit to the school's role for him. Instead he flees the island, launches himself on an unknown world, and burns his modestly single boat.

If all philosophy is a series of footnotes to Plato, it is no insult to say that all writings by educatees of the Irish Jesuits are a series of commentaries on Joyce. Dominic Connolly links arms with Stephen Dedalus, together they shout, *non serviam*, together take boat from their island and together blindly advance into some artistic future that is as much a thing of morality as any code they were ever taught.

Yet Nick Enright's school remains his, not mine. When I went down the drive past the infirmary for the last time, the old Matron was still fiercely alive, and Vietnam was merely the setting for a novel by Graham Greene.

Sydney, 1992

St James Infirmary was first produced by the Q Theatre, Penrith, on 14 February 1992, with the following cast:

JENNY WALSH	Vanessa Downing
FATHER D'ARCY	Ronald Falk
NORMA LOCKWOOD	Glenda Linscott
DOMINIC CONNOLLY	Sam Wilcox
TIM O'DONOHUE	Damon Herriman
BRIAN BOWKER	Felix Nobis

Director, George Ogilvie
Set Designer, Eamon D'Arcy

CHARACTERS

JENNIFER WALSH
NORMA LOCKWOOD
DOMINIC CONNOLLY
TIMOTHY DONOHUE
BRIAN BOWKER
FATHER D'ARCY

SETTING

The play takes place over one week in October, 1967, at St James College, a Catholic boarding school on an island in a river at some distance from a large Australian city.

AUTHOR'S NOTE

This is a substantially revised version of the play *St James Infirmary Blues*, first presented by the students of the National Institute of Dramatic Art at the Parade Theatre in May, 1990, in a production directed by Peter Kingston.

My thanks to NIDA for the opportunity of seeing the earlier version staged; and to all who worked on it there. Grateful thanks to Helmut Bakaitis, Artistic Director of the Q, for his enthusiasm and support; to Rae Davidson and the staff at the Q; to George Ogilvie and his splendid cast and crew; and to the friends and colleagues who have offered advice and help.

The printed text contains further small revisions made for the Melbourne Theatre Company production in April 1993.

ACT ONE

SCENE ONE

Late morning. A room in an old sandstone cottage by a river. In it are three iron beds. One door opens onto a hall. French doors give onto a verandah facing the river. JENNIFER WALSH, *in uniform, holds her veil in her hand. She looks out at the view. Rowing crews call on the water.* FATHER D'ARCY *appears at the hall door, carrying a portfolio.*

D'ARCY: They're pleasant sounds, aren't they?

    She is startled.

    Stroke... stroke... stroke. Regular and comforting. You'll catch every sound across the water. The punt chugging to and fro. Sometimes you can hear bellbirds on the other shore. I'm sorry if I startled you. The front door was wide open.

JENNY: It's warm for October.

D'ARCY: It will get warmer. You'll be grateful for the breeze. And you'll need your mosquito net.

JENNY: [*adjusting her veil*] Excuse me. I can't get this to stay on.

D'ARCY: I doubt you'll need to. There'll be no patients today. It's our last week before swot vac, and the calendar's very full. The art show. The passing-out parade. Prize day. Drama night. They're all too busy to be sick. Enjoy your freedom. We could walk down to the cricket. Or I could show you the library.

JENNY: Thank you. But I'm still settling in, Father...

D'ARCY: D'Arcy.

JENNY: Of course. I beg your pardon.

D'ARCY: Why? You met eighteen men in black. You wouldn't remember all the names. Certainly not mine. I'm very small fry. I'm not even a Division Master.

JENNY: What do you teach, Father?

D'ARCY: Painting and drawing, chiefly. And you can imagine how much status that has. You want to get on with your unpacking.

JENNY: There is some straightening up to do...

D'ARCY: Of course. Things got beyond Matron by the end. But if you could spare me a few minutes, I want to enlist you in a cause.

JENNY: I'm not a great one for causes.

D'ARCY: This one might interest you.

JENNY: Well... what is it?

D'ARCY: The salvation of a soul.

JENNY: Goodness.

D'ARCY: That was a bit over-dramatic, wasn't it? What do I mean? Salvaging, redirection... I don't know. And I'm afraid the Fathers have turned their backs. I've had any number of promising students. But this place being what it is, they go on to be doctors or solicitors or stockbrokers. I've never cared much. They'd need something more than promise to make them artists. But this one boy, Dominic Connolly, he has that. He has a fire in his belly.

JENNY: And a soul that needs saving.

D'ARCY: Well... he's adrift. He needs help. Guidance.

JENNY: What about his mother and father?

D'ARCY: Both dead. Let me show you what he can do. You can throw me out in five minutes. But first. Look, please.

He opens the portfolio.

Time is short. He's only with us for another month. What do you think?

JENNY: Doesn't he have a guardian? Foster-parents?

D'ARCY: His grandparents pay the fees. He's been ours since the age of eleven. And that makes us... makes me feel all the more responsible.

JENNY: For what?

D'ARCY: Up at the college, I'm known as a red-hot liberal. Dangerous D'Arcy. Nudes in the art room, photography, collage. Pop art. And there's worse. I actually encourage the boys to argue and to read. There are usually one or two lively minds that can be fed. And Connolly is the liveliest. [*Showing a bold poster*] Look at this.

JENNY: 'Old soldiers never die. Not while they've got the young ones to do it for them.' Why do you show me this?

D'ARCY: I've set something in motion that I can't control. Last year, he was so hungry. I thought he needed to know something about the world. In the Christmas vacation I arranged for him to take some classes. Partly to sharpen his skills, partly to expose him to other influences. And since then... Well, you'll see. I think you could help him.

JENNY: No.

D'ARCY: You're a stranger. That's important. He's grown to despise the people he knows. Let me bring him down after lunch to meet you.

JENNY: You move quickly, Father.

D'ARCY: I need to. There've been... signs. Meals missed. Chapel skipped. I've been watching. He's become obsessed by this war. Tonight, the Cadet Corps hold their regimental dinner. I think he's planning something. If we could find out what it is...

JENNY: Excuse me. You said 'we'.

D'ARCY: I'm sure he'd take you seriously. I think you could teach him a little discretion.

JENNY: And how would I do that?

D'ARCY: By telling him about what you've seen and done. You could show him there are two sides to every question.

JENNY: There are no two sides to my life. I remember banners like that, the signs hung along the wharves, the slogans they shouted. If he waves a banner tonight, that's his bad luck.

D'ARCY: The loss will be ours as well as his.

JENNY: I haven't come here for this. I've come here to do a job.

D'ARCY: Please let me bring him down here.

> JENNY *picks up the drawings.*

They are good, aren't they? Too good to ignore.

JENNY: Take them away, please.

> NORMA *is heard calling in the hall. She comes in, wearing a*

uniform smock. D'ARCY *leaves one drawing on an empty bed.*

NORMA: Hello? The door was open. I left some supplies in the kitchen.

D'ARCY: Matron Walsh. Mrs Lockwood.

NORMA: Norma.

D'ARCY: You're sure you can't help?

JENNY: Quite sure.

D'ARCY: Enjoy your day, Matron.

He goes.

NORMA: Don't tell me. He's tried to rope you in for the art show. Those priests, they think the world revolves around them. I popped in to see if you've got everything you need. We stocked up before you came.

JENNY: Yes, thank you.

NORMA: And cleared away all the grog bottles. Cartons of them in the laundry. I've brought cheese, and eggs. And enough milk to do you till Monday. I can bring meals down if you like, but I wouldn't recommend it.

JENNY: I think I'll manage.

NORMA: You look like a choosy eater anyway. Not like the old girl, a steady diet of brandy and Craven A's. They were lucky to find you so quick.

JENNY: I'm the lucky one. I needed a job.

NORMA: How long have they got you for?

JENNY: Well... it's open-ended, I hope.

NORMA: Oh.

JENNY: What?

NORMA: I thought this was... temporary. You know, helping them out, till they could find someone...

JENNY: I'm staying. I've got plans already. I'll have the place painted right through. I'll enjoy it here. This view, for one thing.

NORMA: You can get a bit sick of looking out at water. Specially when you can't cross it easy.

JENNY: I'm not thinking about crossing. This is it. I'm here.

NORMA: Won't you go mad with the silence? In daylight you can hear something. The currawongs and the maggies. The regimental band,

4

the rowing crews. But night-times... in a couple of weeks you'll be desperate for the sound of a jack-hammer. Traffic jam. Police siren. Anything but all this peace and quiet.

JENNY: I'm looking forward to that.

NORMA: No. You're too young for it, love... Sorry, I can't call you Matron. Matron still means old Chateau Tanunda. Where'd you leave your car?

JENNY: I didn't. I brought everything up on the train.

NORMA: Mistake number one. Get a little bomb, keep it on the mainland.

JENNY: I'm not about to run away.

NORMA: You'll be wanting to run somewhere.

JENNY: I've more or less burnt my boats.

NORMA: Mistake number two.

JENNY: You seem to be happy enough.

NORMA: I've got a husband on the other side of the water. I'm sorry about yours.

JENNY: What?

NORMA: Your husband. I heard. Stupid, I mean we all did.

JENNY: Yes.

NORMA: Big requiem mass and everything. Now, if there's nothing else you want, I'll look in on Monday.

JENNY *picks up the drawing.*

JENNY: Could you return this to Father D'Arcy? It actually belongs to a boy called...

NORMA: Rembrandt. Connolly. Dominic Connolly. See the signature?

JENNY: Something of an artist, I hear.

NORMA: Something of a lair. Maybe D'Arcy meant you to keep this? It's very nice.

JENNY: No, thanks.

She hands it to NORMA.

NORMA: Won't you be sorry when he wins the Archibald Prize. Okay. I'm off. Enjoy the view. All them rowing crews sliding past your window.

JENNY: My husband was a rower.

NORMA: Yeah. [*Looking out the windows*] Holy Mother of God. It's him.

5

JENNY: What!
NORMA: Rembrandt. Connolly.
JENNY: Connolly?

> NORMA *goes out through the verandah doors.* JENNY *opens them wide.*

Bring him through to the dispensary.

> *She hurries into the hall as* NORMA *and* TIM *enter supporting* DOMINIC. *Both boys wear khaki shorts and shirts and ties.* DOMINIC *is spattered with red. He has a gash down his left thigh. His left temple is grazed.*

NORMA: What happened, Connolly?
TIM: Nothing. Nothing.
DOMINIC: I fell.

> *They carry him out through the hall door. After a moment,* TIM *returns. He examines the stains on his clothes.*

TIM: Oh, God.

> *He starts as he hears* NORMA *calling from the hall. She comes to the door of the ward.*

NORMA: He's lucky he didn't lose that eye. What on earth happened?
TIM: He had a fall. Oh, God. Oh, God.
NORMA: Don't be such a sook. She wants you to go for a doctor.
TIM: Where?
NORMA: Wake up. At the oval.
TIM: The oval?
NORMA: The cricket. There's bound to be one in the stand. Go on, quick! That leg's going to need stitches. Hang on. [*She looks closely at the stains.*] That's not blood. That's paint. What's the story?
TIM: He fell.
NORMA: Into a bucket of paint?

> TIM *runs out the doors. Sounds of pain from the dispensary.* NORMA *goes towards them.*

6

SCENE TWO

DOMINIC *is in bed. The skin around his left eye is discoloured.*
BRIAN BOWKER *enters, dressed in cricket whites.*

BOWKER: You bastard, Connolly. You bastard. God, your eye. Why did
  you do this to me? I had to leave in the middle of the game. And go
  up to the drill-hall and see that. A whole wall spattered with paint.
DOMINIC: I didn't finish.
BOWKER: Nearly a whole wall.
DOMINIC: And not spattered. I thought about it.
BOWKER: That huge thing... what is it?
DOMINIC: A bomb. Exploding on a village. Or it would have been.
BOWKER: It's bullshit.
DOMINIC: It's from a news photo.
BOWKER: And that figure. Is it a woman?
DOMINIC: From another photo. Covered in blood, holding a child.
  Bowker, my head's aching.
BOWKER: You did this to get at my father, didn't you?
DOMINIC: I wanted him to see it.
BOWKER: Well, he's not coming. Ha! He got held up in Canberra. Sorry
  to disappoint you. You're going to pay for this. You and whoever
  helped you. As if I didn't know.
DOMINIC: I was on my own.
BOWKER: There are two sets of footprints in all that paint.
DOMINIC: My head feels like it's had a nail driven through it.
BOWKER: You're lucky you didn't lose that eye. You're bloody mad,
  Dominic. Two weeks before the HSC. Throwing everything away.
  Let alone what you've done to me, you bastard. Bloody bastard!
DOMINIC: Keep it down...
BOWKER: Keep it down. What if I'd stuffed up something for you?
  The art show? Ripped up your little journal? You'd yell your head
  off. Well, you've stuffed up the biggest night of my life.
DOMINIC: Your Dad's not coming.
BOWKER: The Colonel's coming. The Brigadier. The head of Duntroon.
DOMINIC: Old soldiers never die.

7

FATHER D'ARCY *is in the doorway. He is carrying art supplies.*

D'ARCY: Not while they've got young ones to do it for them.

BOWKER: That was just on the wall of the art-room. The wall of the drill-hall is different. It's an outrage.

DOMINIC: In the news photo that woman had the skin burnt off her face. And her baby was dead.

BOWKER: Cut it out! I don't know what to do, Father. There's no time to paint over it. Not before the dinner. It'd take two coats at least. And every one of my officers is on the field or out on the river.

DOMINIC: You've got to be part of a team, boys.

BOWKER: Listen to him now. Last year he was desperate to make the Eight.

DOMINIC: Last year.

BOWKER: This year, this year he gave it all away. Not just rowing. Everything. Football. Debating.

DOMINIC: Debating? I made an open challenge in July. The week of the big bombing raids. The week Cardinal Gilroy blessed the fleet. Nobody would take me on.

BOWKER: That's not debating. You have to be able to take either side.

DOMINIC: Anything to stop you thinking for yourself.

BOWKER: You can't see that other people might do that too? Some of us have good reasons for staying in the Corps.

DOMINIC: Tell him what you played at the August camp. An exercise called Vietcong Village. Skewering straw dummies in the rice-paddies of Singleton. And all in the cause of democracy.

BOWKER: Connolly. I've got to report to Father Rector.

D'ARCY: Mr Bowker. He's in no state to be interrogated.

BOWKER: I've got to have names. Or everyone will suffer.

DOMINIC: But the good guys don't fight that way. Like hell. The Americans bombed a school in Haiphong last week. Killed thirty kids and their teacher.

BOWKER: You didn't do this for school kids. I remember the week the ballot was announced. Three years away from it, and you were terrified your marble might get drawn. That's your politics. Gutlessness and...

D'ARCY: Mr Bowker...

8

BOWKER: And mindless propaganda.

DOMINIC: Please don't yell. My head.

D'ARCY: Mr Bowker, I must talk to Connolly.

BOWKER: My father did a lot for you. Whatever you think of him now. He and Mum were really interested in you.

DOMINIC: I know, Brian.

BOWKER: And you turned your back on them. You insulted him.

D'ARCY: Hadn't you better get back to the oval?

BOWKER: I'll have to go up to college, Father. And try to salvage tonight.

> *He goes.*

D'ARCY: What did his father do for you?

DOMINIC: He took us sailing. Got us into the Members' Stand. He's a nice man. Pity about his party.

D'ARCY: He's only on the back bench. How did you insult him? I suppose you did insult him.

DOMINIC: Christmas morning. I was staying with them at Palm Beach. Brian's little brother was given an aircraft carrier. And I went... well, you know. Off the deep end.

D'ARCY: Dominic, this is the deep end. This morning's effort. The deepest.

DOMINIC: It had a deck full of little fighter bombers, helicopters. All in baby-cack brown.

D'ARCY: Little boys' toys.

> JENNY *comes in.*

DOMINIC: Big boys have toys as well. They had dummy grenades in Vietcong Village.

D'ARCY: Dominic.

DOMINIC: They threw them into huts made out of cardboard. Getting their hate up. Boom! Another village. Another school. Another bunch of slit-eyed gooks get ripped apart.

D'ARCY: Connolly!

JENNY: A message for you. Father Rector would like to see you immediately.

D'ARCY: Thank you, Matron.

> *She goes, closing the door.*

You must not do that. You know she lost her husband in Vietnam?

DOMINIC: I know he was killed.

D'ARCY: You know how?

DOMINIC: He was a captain. And an old boy. That's all I know.

D'ARCY: Father Rector told the story at assembly yesterday.

DOMINIC: I don't go to assemblies.

D'ARCY: They all loved him here. All the older Fathers. Some of them cried when they heard. You must remember the Mass. And the eulogy. Or did you boycott that too?

DOMINIC: Why would I need to go? I could write it. The glorious death of Captain Whatsisname in the battle against godless communism.

D'ARCY: Captain was an honorary title. He was a surgeon. A civilian volunteer. People do, you know. Volunteer, I mean. She was there as well. Though not beside him the day he died, or she'd be dead with him. Is your head getting worse?

DOMINIC: Yes. And my guts are starting to churn.

D'ARCY: Then don't talk. Listen.

DOMINIC: No.

D'ARCY: Last April, he was in a hut in a place called Huong Tra, operating on a South Vietnamese infantryman. The hut was blown up by the Vietcong. Torn limb from limb... sounds like a clean process. But they were turned into pulp and gristle. At least she was spared the business of identification. They found his name-tag eventually.

DOMINIC: The Vietcong are fighting for their country.

D'ARCY: They killed their own countryman. As well as two of ours. And with a bomb that was made in China.

DOMINIC: What's that got to do with anything!

D'ARCY: It may show you that there are two sides to every question. Dominic, you'll be expelled. The one thing that might save you would be a public apology.

DOMINIC: I think I'm going to chuck...

D'ARCY: Listen. If you are expelled, what will happen to you?

DOMINIC: I need a bucket.

D'ARCY: What will you do?

DOMINIC: What I always said I'd do. Go to art school.

D'ARCY: Not without your HSC. And it's too late for you to sit anywhere else. So you'd waste a year, an important year. And where? Back on Norfolk Island with your grandparents?

DOMINIC: No! I'll get a job.

D'ARCY: Not much fun. Cut off from so much you'll need.

DOMINIC: Cut off? This island is cut off. Out there...

D'ARCY: Out there, you'd have no money, no equipment, no space.

DOMINIC: I'd get money. Rent a room. I can do anything. Work in a factory.

D'ARCY: You wouldn't last ten minutes.

DOMINIC: Get me a bucket, please.

D'ARCY: If you go, Dominic, I discard you. No, you cut yourself off.

DOMINIC: Okay. Look, my guts—

D'ARCY: None of us want you to go. Not this way. And if you'll make some apology—

DOMINIC: No. I'm sorry for one thing. Only one thing. I didn't finish it.

D'ARCY: That mural is ugly and stupid.

DOMINIC: Like the war.

D'ARCY: It's bad art—

DOMINIC: You say.

D'ARCY: And bad politics. Worse than that. It's fake. You know why? It's all about displaying your sensibilities. It has nothing to do with the truth of the matter.

DOMINIC: It's based on news photos.

D'ARCY: Nobody was there to photograph the death of Doctor Walsh. And nobody got the pictures of his mates puking as they filled the body bag. Could you paint that? Blood and guts. Pulp and gristle.

> DOMINIC *lurches out of bed and hobbles towards the door, retching.* D'ARCY *stays still as* DOMINIC *vomits in the hall.*

JENNY: [*off*] Why didn't you call? Into the bathroom, quick...

> TIM *is at the verandah doors, peering in.*

TIM: Oh. Father. I... heard Connolly was here.

D'ARCY: You heard that, did you, Donohue?

TIM: Yes, Father.

D'ARCY: How all occasions inform against you, Donohue.

TIM: What? Oh. Yes. We mightn't be doing that bit. Where's Connolly, Father?

D'ARCY: Do you think you'll make a good Hamlet, Donohue?

TIM: I hope so, Father. Is he here, Father?

D'ARCY: Somehow I see you more as Horatio. On your way, Donohue.

TIM: Father... yes, Father.

He goes as JENNY *looks in from the hall. She holds clean pyjamas.* D'ARCY *indicates the art materials.*

D'ARCY: I'll leave these for him. He's recovering?

JENNY: Yes. You could have helped him, Father.

D'ARCY: I think now he's ready to be helped... by both of us.

JENNY: I'll look after his leg and his eye and the bruises on his ribs. The rest of him is your department.

D'ARCY: Please. I can't do this alone. I'm too compromised. I'll get no support from the Fathers. I need your help.

JENNY: Excuse me.

She goes. He puts the art materials by the bed, and goes out through the garden.

SCENE THREE

Afternoon. DOMINIC *is in bed, with his sketching block. His eye is livid. There is a walking-stick beside the bed.* TIM *creeps into the room from the verandah.*

TIM: I love the eye.

DOMINIC: Oh. Good.

TIM: I've been hanging round down by the willows. Watching.

A distant bell rings.

Oh, shit, the refectory bell. That's half an hour early. I would have come in sooner, but every time I've tried, there's been someone else. It's like a railway station. Dangerous D'Arcy. Doctor Lenane. Father Rector. What did he say?

DOMINIC: He stood there shaking his head. 'Oh, Connolly'...

TIM: 'Oh, Connolly'...

DOMINIC: ... he said he'd rung my grandparents, and they were shocked of course, but they were leaving the matter in his hands, and why

12

did I do it, and who put me up to it, and what about my HSC, and who was with me?

TIM: Did you tell him?

DOMINIC: Oh, come on, Tim.

TIM: But I want them to know.

DOMINIC: Eh?

TIM: If you're going, I'm going too. I did help.

DOMINIC: You stood and watched.

TIM: I passed you up the paint. If you'd told me beforehand I could have done more... helped you plan it.

DOMINIC: Why would I tell you?

TIM: Because it's important.

DOMINIC: Important to me, maybe.

TIM: Anyway, I was with you.

DOMINIC: You followed me in.

TIM: I'm in it with you. I wish I could finish it for you.

DOMINIC: What about your play? You'd lose that if they sacked you.

TIM: There'll be plays outside. If you're sacked I'm with you.

DOMINIC: Oh, mate. You're sixteen. Your old man would put the cops after you and drag you back home.

TIM: I'm never going back to Goulburn. And anyway, you're only seventeen.

DOMINIC: I'm eighteen next week. I'm a free man.

TIM: Let me come with you. Let me. Please.

DOMINIC: You've got to watch that whining. You do it in your plays, too. It sounds weak.

TIM: What do you know about acting? You don't know everything about everything.

DOMINIC: Listen. This is the story. I came out of the drill-hall and you saw me, and helped me down here. No-one can call you a liar. They were all at the rowing or the cricket.

TIM: No. I'm sick of lying. I want to say what I was doing. This is mine as well. You want to believe you did it alone.

DOMINIC: It doesn't matter who did it. The statement's there.

TIM: Not all of it.

DOMINIC: Enough. They'll see it. They can't paint over it. They haven't got time.

BOWKER *is at the hall door in his cadet Adjutant's uniform.*

BOWKER: That's right. We can't paint over it, so we've moved the dinner. To the refectory.

DOMINIC: Away from all the flags and trophy-cases?

BOWKER: We're moving the flags and trophy-cases. I've left it to the CUO's. A new kind of field manoeuvre. I had tea brought forward. By seven-thirty the ref will be set up. Your efforts have been wasted, Connolly. And yours, Donohue.

DOMINIC: He wasn't involved.

BOWKER: What did you do while he was up the ladder? Reel off a bit of Shakespeare?

DOMINIC: He wasn't there.

BOWKER: His khakis were covered in red paint.

TIM: How do you know?

BOWKER: I searched your locker.

TIM: You shit.

BOWKER: They don't say that in Shakespeare. Donohue's Hamlet. That'll be something to see. Who were you last year? You wore a big pink dress with a fan.

TIM: Lydia Languish.

BOWKER: Lydia Languish. And now Hamlet. That's a step up. Hamlet, the Prince of Goulburn.

TIM: Denmark! I'll be good, too.

BOWKER: You'll need to be. How much of it are they doing?

TIM: Just the key scenes. Father Mac's cut out a lot.

BOWKER: Too bad if he's got to cut out the Prince.

The bell rings again.

Second bell, Donohue. You're late for tea. Hang on. Hands. I thought your kind liked to keep yourselves neat? There's paint under your fingernails.

DOMINIC *swings at* BOWKER *with his stick.* BOWKER *swerves to avoid the blow.*

Never attack from flat on your back. Go, Donohue.

TIM: You're a fascist bastard, Bowker.

DOMINIC: Tim...

TIM: He is. He's always raiding my locker. He confiscated my picture of Vanessa Redgrave. 'That's a pin-up', he said. A pin-up! She's a great actress. And a pacifist.

BOWKER: Rules are rules, Donohue. Even for actresses. And clean your nails. After tea. Off you go.

TIM *goes.*

Fascist bastard. A year ago he wouldn't have known what that meant. You've done a real job on him.

DOMINIC: He wasn't involved.

BOWKER: He hasn't denied it himself. And anything you're in he's in. You should have stayed in the Regiment. You could have had a whole platoon following you instead of just Donohue.

DOMINIC: I don't want followers.

BOWKER: I've seen you all this year, ear-bashing anyone you thought would listen. And no-one would. Now you've got yourself expelled, and all for what? A bit of vandalism that no-one will see.

DOMINIC: They will. Maybe not tonight. But they'll see.

BOWKER: They won't. The doors are locked. And tomorrow morning, Kev Lockwood will be in there with the rollers.

DOMINIC: Still, they'll hear what was up there.

BOWKER: But they won't get it. I know more about your politics than anyone, and even then you had to explain it to me.

DOMINIC: It's a simple statement.

BOWKER: It's paint on a wall. And tomorrow it'll be covered over. You know my mother thinks you've got real talent? She was sorry you pulled away from us. She'll be really sorry you've thrown it all in. I'm going down to the punt. The band's going to march the visitors up to college. This is my night. And there's nothing you can do now. No more statements, no more chance to make them.

DOMINIC: There's the passing-out parade.

BOWKER: That's a week away. You'll be well gone by then. I don't reckon we'll be talking again, Connolly. Good luck. I'd better get down to the jetty. We've got a big night ahead of us.

He goes out across the verandah as NORMA *enters with a tray.*

NORMA: Hungry? You'll need to be to get through this. A delicious stew of old rugby boots.

15

DOMINIC: Normie, will you get me some crutches?

NORMA: Boy, you're lucky you're safe in bed. Kev wants a piece of your hide.

DOMINIC: Kev and me are mates.

NORMA: Not any more. He's ropable. Getting into his sacred paint-store, ruining his brushes, smashing up his ladder. And who's going to have to clean all that paint off the floor? Oh, yes, and I've got a bone to pick with you, too, Rembrandt. Another little art-work. The one of me and Kev in the nuddy.

DOMINIC: I wondered where that had got to.

NORMA: It got to me.

DOMINIC: Make you laugh?

NORMA: Like a drain. I don't know whether Kev'll be so amused. Specially now. Why'd you put us in the bath?

DOMINIC: It felt right.

NORMA: It is right. We hop in together. Every now and then. Well, every Sunday night. I thought you must be a peeping Tom.

DOMINIC: Normie, I need crutches.

> *The band starts to play by the river.*

NORMA: There you go. Music to chew by. The bugle boys down by the jetty.

> *Drum-roll.*

That's the big brass, coming in on the punt.

> *Fanfare.*

That Bowker, he's making all the right moves.

DOMINIC: I need some crutches!

> *But* NORMA *is gone. The band passes.* DOMINIC *tries to get out of bed, knocking his tray to the floor.*

DOMINIC: Shit.

> JENNY *appears.*

JENNY: What was that?

DOMINIC: I lost my dinner.

JENNY: Did you vomit again?

DOMINIC: Give me a chance. I hadn't eaten.

16

JENNY *cleans up the food.*

Can I have some crutches?

JENNY: No. You're to rest that leg.

DOMINIC: Please?

JENNY: I'll bring you a bottle if you need to...

DOMINIC: I need some crutches!

JENNY: You're to lie there and rest.

> *She goes with the tray.*

DOMINIC: Shit. Shit. Shit.

> *He grabs his stick, gets up and hobbles out the verandah*
> *door. The music swells.* JENNY *returns with a mop and bucket.*
> *She sees he has gone, and hurries out the verandah doors.*

JENNY: [*off*] Connolly! Connolly, come back here! [*She puts him back*
to bed, checking his injuries.] There are stitches in this leg. How
dare you leave this ward!

DOMINIC: Listen to that. I should be out there.

JENNY: I'll have to lock the doors.

DOMINIC: No!

JENNY: Then promise you'll stay put.

DOMINIC: Promise.

> *She mops. The music fades as the band moves on.*

I'm hungry.

JENNY: You threw your dinner away.

DOMINIC: Even prisoners of war get fed. That's the Geneva Convention.

JENNY: You don't know the first thing about war.

DOMINIC: 'And it'd be a damn good thing for you if you did.'

JENNY: Don't put me in a box. Don't label me.

> *Silence.*

Are you in pain?

> DOMINIC *nods, turning his head away from her.*

Serves you right. Why do you keep on...? Oh, for goodness sake,
don't cry.

DOMINIC: I'm not. I just feel crook.

JENNY: What were you trying to do, anyway?

DOMINIC: I don't know. Cross their path some way.

JENNY: Why?

DOMINIC: Why do you think? To make some sort of statement. They keep telling us we're an intellectual community. It's named after a rebel, you know.

Silence.

I said named after a rebel. A poet.

JENNY: What is?

DOMINIC: This place. St James Northcott. Poet and martyr. A man of intellect who died for his convictions. And he's our model. You understand? They make us learn the details by heart. He was wounded in battle against the Spanish in the Netherlands. In hospital he had a mystical rebirth. Christ spoke to the soldier, through a sparrow on the window-ledge. He was converted, joined the J's, went back to England as a kind of Catholic undercover man. Christ's corporal, he called himself. Lived in hiding for three years. Priests' holes, the whole bit. Wrote a long poem called *The Sparrow's Discourse.* It's good, too. He was caught after the Gunpowder Plot. Hanged at Tyburn in 1606. And Bowker's off to Duntroon next year.

JENNY: I don't follow the logic of that.

DOMINIC: Because there isn't any.

She adjusts her veil.

Can I draw you, Matron?

JENNY: I beg your pardon?

DOMINIC: I'd like to draw you. Woman having trouble with veil.

JENNY: I'll get you some food. It will only be a sandwich. And a cup of tea?

DOMINIC: Coffee. Black, no sugar. You're impressed.

JENNY: Am I?

DOMINIC: Your eyebrows went up.

JENNY: That may be a nervous tic. You can have Milo. Or is that beneath contempt in the circles you move in?

DOMINIC: Tea, thanks. And then I'd like to draw you. It would take the pain away.

JENNY: I'll get you some aspirin.

DOMINIC: Please.

JENNY: It's not appropriate, Connolly.

DOMINIC: You don't have to stick to surnames. I'm Dominic. And you're Jennifer.

JENNY: Not to you. How do you know that?

DOMINIC: Your nursing certificate. It was on the dispensary table. Do you frame it and hang it like a barber?

The phone rings in the hall.

Do they call you Jenny?

JENNY *goes to answer the phone, leaving the door open.* DOMINIC *starts to sketch, straining to overhear the call.*

JENNY: [*off*] Hello?... Yes, Father... Yes, Father... When is that?... I'd like to think about that... Yes, I will. Thank you, Father.

DOMINIC: [*calling*] Was that the Rector? [*Silence. He calls louder.*] The Rector. It was, wasn't it?

JENNY *appears at the door.*

JENNY: Yes, it was. If it's any business of yours.

DOMINIC: Funny. Everyone sounds the same speaking to him. 'Yes, Father. Yes, Father. I'd like to think about that, Father.'

JENNY *turns to go.*

JENNY: Do you take milk?

DOMINIC: Was it about me?

JENNY: No. Milk and sugar?

DOMINIC: It was, wasn't it?

JENNY: You're not the only topic of interest in this school. It was about the passing-out parade.

DOMINIC: The passing-out parade... He wants you to be on the dais. Doesn't he? Perfect. The perfect statement.

JENNY: I haven't been asked to speak.

DOMINIC: Being there, that's the statement.

JENNY: What do you want on your sandwich? Cheese? Tomato?

DOMINIC: Thanks.

JENNY *goes out, but returns immediately.*

JENNY: Look! Why do you think people, good, sensible people, choose to serve in wars?

DOMINIC: Most of them don't choose. Their marble gets drawn out of a barrel.

JENNY: Oh! That's what's behind this. You're scared of being conscripted!

DOMINIC: No. But I think it's immoral. The ballot, I mean. Just because this Government wants Australia to be a lackey of the USA... [*Ignoring her groans*] ... in a war of imperialist aggression.

JENNY: I looked you up in last year's magazine. You seemed to be on every second page. Rowing and rugby and debating—

DOMINIC: All the really important things.

JENNY: They were important. I could tell it in your face. Very important. And the oratory prize. And the art show. Achievement all round. And you've thrown it all away. Who got to you?

DOMINIC: Nobody got to me. I've read a bit, that's all.

JENNY: Somebody got to you. It was over Christmas, wasn't it?

DOMINIC: You've found out a lot in one afternoon.

JENNY: Father D'Arcy told me. He sent you to some classes.

DOMINIC: Not classes, a workshop. Art and Society: An Introduction. We did everything. Collage. Posters. Screen-printing. Photography. A bit of film-making.

JENNY: And a lot of talking.

DOMINIC: They taught us it's the content that matters. The statement. Finding the best way to say something.

JENNY: You'd never heard that here?

DOMINIC: Are you kidding? This woman opened my eyes. Martha Herzfeld. She was on the streets of Sydney the day of LBJ's motorcade. Bastards' Day, she called it. You know, drive over the bastards. She was one of the bastards. She got it all on film.

JENNY: On the streets of Sydney. Was she ever on the streets of Saigon?

DOMINIC: I don't know.

JENNY: Yes, you do. Da Nang? Nui Dat? Has she ever been there, this Martha Herzberg?

DOMINIC: Feld. Herzfeld. She's very well-known.

JENNY: Has she been to the war, seen the country?

DOMINIC: No, I don't think so.

JENNY: But she knows what's going on there. And she taught you to say 'lackey' and 'imperialist' and—

DOMINIC: She didn't teach us anything. Except about the connection between art and the world.

JENNY: Old soldiers never die. Not while they have young ones...

DOMINIC: ...to do it for them. It's true. Bowker's Colonel, his Brigadier, Father Rector, they turn seventeen-year-old boys into soldiers. Bowker's off to Duntroon. He could die. He could kill. He's worth more than that. How did you see that poster?

JENNY: Father D'Arcy showed me. You're causing him a lot of pain, you know.

DOMINIC: Pain. D'Arcy lent me a book once. *The Naked And The Dead.* The Division Master found it in my locker. He'd never read it, never even heard of it, but he knew it was immoral. I got six on the behind. And Dangerous never spoke up for me. That's how this place works. It's a police state with pretensions. You'll see. Tell me why you're here.

JENNY: Is it any of your business?

DOMINIC: I've told you things. Are you just filling in?

JENNY: Everyone asks me that.

DOMINIC: Because you don't look like a matron.

JENNY: Perhaps I don't look like the last matron.

DOMINIC: You don't. No moustache, for one thing.

JENNY: But I am here to stay.

DOMINIC: Why? Is this a kind of retreat?

JENNY: This is my profession. I need to work.

DOMINIC: Not here you don't.

JENNY: Here.

DOMINIC: How long for? The old one drank herself to death, you know. She was violent. Started seeing things.

JENNY: Give me time, Connolly.

      DOMINIC *laughs, winces.*

Ribs?

DOMINIC: Neck.

JENNY: You want it rubbed?

DOMINIC: Oh, yes.

JENNY: Only if you promise to shut up.

DOMINIC: Promise.

Silence as she works his neck.

I know why you came.

JENNY: Shut up!

DOMINIC: It's the dead hero's resting place.

JENNY: He doesn't rest here.

DOMINIC: In spirit. There'll be a plaque in the chapel before long. Or on the boat-shed. The Vikings used to burn theirs. Their boats, I mean. Put the warrior out to sea. Ouch. That's hard. I've gone too far, haven't I?

JENNY: I don't know which is worse, your rudeness, or your smugness when you apologise. If that was an apology.

DOMINIC: It was. Sorry. Sorry if I've been a bit of a shit. Oh. Sorry for saying shit. You know that joke? The little nun? Burns herself with the iron? Oh, shit. Oh, bugger it, I said shit. Oh, fuckit, I didn't want to be a nun anyway.

JENNY is laughing.

That's good. Thank you. Oh. Yes.

He tries to kiss her. She breaks away. Silence.

JENNY: I can't report you, can I? You're on your way out. You can do what you like.

DOMINIC: That's not why...

JENNY: I'll get you some food.

DOMINIC: Jenny—

JENNY: It's Matron. Matron Walsh.

DOMINIC: Look... I was just trying to say something.

JENNY: Yes. I know what it was.

She goes.

SCENE FOUR

Night. The moon is up. DOMINIC *sketches by the light of a bedside lamp. Beside his bed is a half-eaten sandwich and a cup.* BOWKER *appears at the verandah doors, still in uniform.*

BOWKER: I just wanted you to know...

DOMINIC: The night was a triumph.

BOWKER: The refectory looked great. The Colonel was happy. I wish Dad had been there. Yes, it was a triumph.

DOMINIC: You're drunk. Aren't you? Yes, you are. Oh, Bowker.

BOWKER: We're allowed to have a drink at the Regimental Dinner. Why do you hate me so much? Dominic?

DOMINIC: Go away, Bowker. Piss off.

BOWKER: No. Not till—

DOMINIC: You've delivered your message. A triumph for the mighty Corps. How did the evening end? Another round of Viet Cong Village? A midnight dorm raid with a few canisters of napalm?

BOWKER: I asked you a question. Answer my question.

DOMINIC: What was it?

BOWKER: You heard. I said why do you hate me? You lit up inside. Call yourself a pacifist, but you get a real thrill from that.

DOMINIC: From what?

BOWKER: Hurting people. Me. Hurting me. All this year. Last year, last year we were mates. Exeat weekends, the footie, the beach house, my mother's gallery... you loved it all. We were like... we could have been brothers. You and my Dad and me, in the Members' Stand for the Grand Final. The best times. I felt... Oh, Christ...

He crumples, perhaps crying. DOMINIC *watches, motionless.*

Then the Christmas holidays, something happened.

DOMINIC: Yes.

BOWKER: What? What happened?

DOMINIC: Things.

BOWKER: Things you couldn't tell me?

DOMINIC: No.

BOWKER: Tell me now. What happened to us?

DOMINIC: Okay, Brian, I'll try and explain. Are you okay? Brian?

He touches BOWKER, *who recoils abruptly.*

BOWKER: None of that. I'm not Donohue.

DOMINIC: What do you mean?

BOWKER: You know.

DOMINIC: What?

BOWKER: Don't make me say it.

DOMINIC: Say it.

BOWKER: You know! I've seen things.

DOMINIC: Seen what?

BOWKER: I know what goes on. You and him. I don't know why you waste your time.

DOMINIC: Tim's all right. He's a good friend.

BOWKER: Some friend. Some friend you are. You've ruined his school career. You'll get him sacked.

DOMINIC: He wasn't involved.

BOWKER: He's in it. You beckoned and he followed. And that's the way you like it, isn't it?

DOMINIC: People do what they want to do.

BOWKER: Your people do what you want them to do. You, you're so down on the Regiment. All those speeches. Imperialist... whatever. Armed invasion... But you've taken over Donohue, heart and soul. I call that armed invasion.

DOMINIC: How would you know?

BOWKER: Because you did it to me. You take people's feelings and turn them into something you can use.

DOMINIC: I never asked you to be my friend, Bowker.

BOWKER: I must have heard wrong.

He sees what DOMINIC *is drawing.*

This is a nude. God. It's the Matron. Did you do this out of your head?

DOMINIC: What do you think!

BOWKER: God.

DOMINIC: What? What!

BOWKER: Well, it's... good. It's... [*He wants to say 'beautiful'.*] I didn't know you did stuff like this. Listen, Dominic. I'll show this to my mother. She knows about all this. She could... you know, take you under her wing. Next year. My father could fix things here. Tell you what. You apologise, show them you're ready to knuckle down, and I swear you'd get off with a beating. Six on each hand, six on the arse. They'll have to go that far, this is not just smoking behind the handball courts, you've done something pretty major. But I know they wouldn't sack you if Mum and Dad got behind you...

DOMINIC: No.

BOWKER: You can't just leave, go back to Norfolk Island...

DOMINIC: There's no danger of that. No more islands.

BOWKER: Then you'll be out in the world. And you'll need your HSC. Don't fool yourself, you will. And you'll need friends. My parents could do—

DOMINIC: No. Thanks. But no.

BOWKER: Think about it.

DOMINIC: No. I can't go in the Members' Stand any more, Brian.

BOWKER: You stupid arrogant bastard.

He runs out across the verandah, taking the drawing.

DOMINIC: Don't take that. Bowker! Give it back! [*He struggles to the doors.*] Give it back!

A light goes on in the hall. JENNY *appears in a dressing-gown.*

JENNY: What's this noise? What's going on?

DOMINIC: Nothing. A bad dream.

JENNY: Do you always dream standing up? Back to bed. Lie there. And sleep. What was the dream?

DOMINIC: I lost something. Something beautiful.

JENNY: Well, go to sleep. Perhaps you'll get it back.

She goes, turning out the light in the hall.

SCENE FIVE

Morning. DOMINIC*'s bed is empty.* JENNY *makes it. She picks up his sketch-pad, opens it and studies a drawing.* NORMA *enters with a tray, startling her.*

NORMA: Morning, Matron. Where's Rembrandt?

JENNY: Connolly? In the bathroom. He insisted he could manage on his own.

NORMA: And how was your first night? Not too quiet for you? The old girl hated the silence. Kev and me are on the mainland, straight

25

through them trees, and the nights she was on the turps, which was more nights than not, you'd hear her across the water, up 'till all hours, playing the gramophone. All the old jazz numbers. Black-and-white Boogie, Stomping at the Savoy, Kitten On The Keys. But she never played the obvious one. St James Infirmary Blues. Anyway, she never would have seen the joke. Still sure you're going to stay?

JENNY: Well, yes.

NORMA: After twenty-four hours locked up with Connolly? He's been a handful, hasn't he? I could have warned you. More hide than Jessie. Kev's up in the drill-hall with the rollers. And on his day off. It's going to take him ages. It's one thing to spray a wall with red paint. It's another thing to cover it up, so as you can't see what's underneath. Three coats minimum, he reckons. But that's his orders. All because of Connolly and his bright ideas. Kev's ready to kill him. Of course, he'll be joining a long queue. You look a bit off-colour, love. Did you sleep at all?

JENNY: Till about five. I got up and went to early Mass. I'm all right, thanks, Norma.

NORMA: You should see his real masterpiece. Rembrandt's, not Kev's. It's the two of us in the bath. Not drawn from life, of course, but a bloody good likeness. Though if I was set up that well, I'd be on the cover of *Pix*. And if Kev was set up that well, he'd be in a sideshow. Look, how about I cook you up a good big breakfast?

JENNY: No, thank you.

NORMA: You're not one of those diet maniacs, are you? Don't do it to yourself. Eggs, sausages, fried tomatoes, I'm going to give you the works.

JENNY: Truly, I'm fine.

NORMA: You make a good bed. The way they run this place... Up there at college, they have those long cold dormitories, stone walls and bare light-bulbs and not a decent bit of carpet or a pair of curtains to warm the place up, but they've got the school crest woven into the bedspreads. See? Some poor old nun went blind doing that, I'll bet. A sword and a sparrow and a big motto. *Semper Audax*.

FATHER D'ARCY *is in the hall doorway. They do not see him till he speaks.*

26

JENNY: What does that mean?

NORMA: Search me.

D'ARCY: Always bold. Always daring.

NORMA: Well, there you go, Father. One mystery solved. *Semper Audax*. Good name for a race-horse.

D'ARCY: It's for St James. It's the Northcott family motto.

NORMA: Still a good name for a horse. *Semper Audax*. You'd feel safe putting your money on that. I'm going to cook you that breakfast. And I'm going to stand over you while you eat it.

She goes.

JENNY: No, please...

D'ARCY: Don't argue. She sees herself as mother to the world.

JENNY: Then why didn't you ask her to talk to Connolly?

D'ARCY: I think you'd do better.

JENNY: I'm not in this. I'm not his mother.

D'ARCY: He lost his mother when he was four.

JENNY: I'm not going to be made responsible—

D'ARCY: No-one ever said you would be. But if he had a woman close to him, someone he might trust and listen to...

JENNY: Why did you think it's a woman he needs?

D'ARCY: Because of the way he draws. It shows what he sees in women, and what he sees in men. And I thought a woman like yourself, who'd witnessed things that Dominic's only read about...

JENNY: War, you mean? You can say the word.

D'ARCY: I mean violence. There's a strain of it emerging in him, in his work. He hates it in himself, and he turns that to a hatred of war, this war. And so he takes the side of the victim, like that woman on the wall. You saw it this morning, I hear. A gross simplification. You could show him that the real issues are complex.

JENNY: You can't use people like that, Father.

D'ARCY: Do you know how much I love this boy? [*Pause.*] No. Not in that way. I love what's in him. What he can become.

The phone rings in the hall.

JENNY: Excuse me.

D'ARCY: Let Norma get it. [*He calls to* NORMA, *and closes the door as she answers the phone.*] I need your help.

27

JENNY: You have to let things take their course. If he's going to be any good, Father—

D'ARCY: You've seen the work. You know he'll be good.

JENNY: Then he'll survive anyway. They can't make an exception of him. He'll have to go.

D'ARCY: There's another possibility.

> NORMA *comes in.*

NORMA: It's for you, Father. Lady Hopcroft.

D'ARCY: Oh...

NORMA: They switched the call through from the common room.

D'ARCY: May I... take it in the dispensary?

> JENNY *nods. He goes.*

NORMA: Lady Hopcroft drives a bashed-up old Bentley with an Alsatian in the back seat.

JENNY: Hopcroft. I know that name.

NORMA: The plaque on the doors of the library. She had it done over in memory of her husband. He's the big portrait in the corridor. They've hung it where all his medals catch the morning sun.

JENNY: Hopcroft. No, it's something else.

> DOMINIC *comes in.*

NORMA: You took your time.

DOMINIC: I fell asleep in the bath.

NORMA: Don't mention bath to me, Rembrandt. Look, your breakfast is stone cold. And I'm not fetching you another one.

DOMINIC: There's hot food cooking down the hall. Smells great.

NORMA: Oh, crikey.

> *She is going.*

JENNY: Give it to Connolly. Truly, Norma, I'm not hungry.

DOMINIC: I am.

NORMA: Thank you, Matron.

DOMINIC: Thank you, Matron.

NORMA: Your manners, boy.

DOMINIC: Give it a rest, Normie.

NORMA: Uh! It's Mrs Lockwood to you from here on in. No more Normie, and no more Kev. My mate Kev. You've cost him his day

28

off. And I'd got him lined up to take the kids into Gosford for a go on the water slide. So there'll no more arvo teas with Kev and Normie, no more beers and smokes on the quiet. You're running out of friends fast, Rembrandt.

She hurries out. JENNY *helps* DOMINIC *back to bed.*

JENNY: She's been pretty good to you.

DOMINIC: Yes.

JENNY: How did you get over there?

DOMINIC: Kev got a new dinghy and gave me the old one. I keep it hidden down by Castle Rock. I muck around in it after dark.

JENNY: Not such a miserable life.

DOMINIC: If I was seen in daylight, the boat would be confiscated, and I'd be thrashed, okay? Only the rowing crews are allowed on the water. Everyone else uses the punt. You'll get to know all the rules, Matron.

D'ARCY *returns.* JENNY *picks up the tray.*

JENNY: I'll bring you something hot.

She goes.

D'ARCY: How is your head?

DOMINIC: Clearer.

D'ARCY: Good. I want you to listen quietly, and say nothing till I've finished.

DOMINIC: I'm going, Father. They can sack me as soon as these stitches are out.

D'ARCY: Nothing is fixed. Listen!

DOMINIC: I'm going.

D'ARCY: Exactly. So listen. There are places you can go where you'll find what you need. Pictures, galleries, old work, new work. And people. Teachers, innovators. It may be London, or Paris, or New York... I don't know, I've never seen those places. But you can.

DOMINIC: Yes. I'll get there. When I save some money.

D'ARCY: There is money. Enough to get you overseas. And keep you there while you study.

DOMINIC: There are no art scholarships.

D'ARCY: No. But there is the Hopcroft.

DOMINIC: The Hopcroft?

D'ARCY: It could be yours.

DOMINIC: That's for doctors and scientists.

D'ARCY: The money is to help an outstanding College man to develop his capacities for the good of the community. That has always meant something like clinical pathology or irrigation systems. But it can mean painting and drawing.

DOMINIC: If you stretch a point.

D'ARCY: The conditions allow it. The decision is Lady Hopcroft's.

DOMINIC: But she takes advice from Father Rector.

D'ARCY: Among others. The decision is hers.

DOMINIC: Nobody gives scholarships to people who get sacked.

D'ARCY: You haven't been sacked.

DOMINIC: Only because I'm stuck here.

D'ARCY: Nothing's decided.

DOMINIC: Come on. Father Rector was down here. He had steam coming out of his nostrils.

D'ARCY: Bowker moved so quickly. Scarcely anyone saw what you did. It'll be gone by tonight. Lady Hopcroft need never know. I've shown her a great deal of your work. Yesterday I asked her for a decision.

DOMINIC: And?

D'ARCY: She'll have to talk to Father Rector. But she knows there are really only two other candidates.

DOMINIC: There's only two, period. It'll be Fitzgerald. He's the big brain. Or Bowker. He's the leader.

D'ARCY: Fitzgerald's people have got pots of money. And Bowker's off to Duntroon.

DOMINIC: Father Rector's not going to buy this. You don't reward people for bucking the system. You sack them.

D'ARCY: He could be persuaded that you're a special case. An artist in the making. But there'd have to be a sign of grace.

DOMINIC: No apologies.

D'ARCY: A sign of grace.

DOMINIC: What does that mean?

D'ARCY: Tell me this first. Do you want it? Paris or London or New York?

DOMINIC: Who wouldn't?

D'ARCY: Then you could offer the school something. The Rector thinks you're very gifted. Unruly and incomprehensible. But gifted.

> JENNY *brings hot food.*

If I told him that you'd wait back after the HSC—

DOMINIC: What?

D'ARCY: Just for a few days. Wait back and paint something for the school...

DOMINIC: Paint what?

D'ARCY: I think it should be a mural.

DOMINIC: Oh, come on!

D'ARCY: For the library corridor. Father Rector has a special passion for the life of—

DOMINIC: St James Northcott.

D'ARCY: Christ's corporal, they call him, Matron. He was the first of our English martyrs to be canonised. 1886, the year the Fathers were given this island to start their school.

JENNY: Yes, Father. [*To* DOMINIC] Don't let this get cold.

> *She goes.*

DOMINIC: St James Northcott. I've had six years of him.

D'ARCY: Then you know what a subject he'd make.

DOMINIC: I won't do it. I can't paint to order.

D'ARCY: It's been done before. Giotto, Della Francesca, Leonardo, they all painted to order. And if it meant that you'd get to see them, up close... Any of them. Your eyes will open. Raphael and Goya and Turner. Cezanne and Picasso and—

DOMINIC: All your favourites.

D'ARCY: And Diego Rivera, who's yours. And Bacon and de Kooning and Rothko, and people you and I have never heard of. The names aren't the point. You'll find your own. It's all there for you. Don't say any more. Think. Think about Europe.

> JENNY *returns.*

Think. And eat. I'll come back this afternoon.

> *He goes.* DOMINIC *starts devouring the food.*

JENNY: Do you want tea with that?

DOMINIC: Thank you. This is good. Thanks.

JENNY: Norma cooked it. Don't eat so fast. [*She is going, but stops.*] Hopcroft. Of course. It's not just the library. It's a scholarship. Isn't it? Luke won it. And they're going to offer it to you?

> *Silence.*

Will you take it? Europe, he said.

> *Silence.*

I went up to early mass this morning. I asked Father Rector to show me the drill-hall. To see what you'd done, or what you'd started. I thought I'd hate it. But I didn't. Even unfinished it was... well, it was powerful. It showed what you felt. And you were prepared to stand by it.

DOMINIC: I still am.

JENNY: No. Father D'Arcy's going to make it all right for you, isn't he?

DOMINIC: How do you know that?

JENNY: I saw him go out the front door just now. It's the first time I've seen him happy. They'll get you to paint the corridor outside the library. And his skin will be saved because yours is. He'll get you the Hopcroft scholarship. Does Lady Hopcroft know what you did in the drill-hall? Does she?

> *Pause.* DOMINIC *shakes his head.*

Will she? Will they tell her?

> DOMINIC *shakes his head.*

No, of course not. Not the widow of a war hero. Brigadier-General Hopcroft.

DOMINIC: Oh, Christ.

JENNY: You hadn't thought that far, had you? But does it change anything?

DOMINIC: I have to think.

JENNY: No. It's simple. You painted one wall. But now you want the prize. So now you'll paint another wall.

> *She goes out of the room.* DOMINIC *is out of bed. Suddenly he grabs a tube of red acrylic paint, sprays it violently on the wall. A beat, then he clambers up onto the bed with difficulty, and starts to smear the paint into a pattern, working it with his fingers and palms.*

ACT TWO

SCENE ONE

DOMINIC *stands on his bed, finishing the wall-picture, a contorted male figure in a circle, holding some sort of weapon.* TIM *appears at the verandah doors.*

TIM: Oh, God. Oh, God. Oh, God. What is it? It's a man. It's fantastic. Like dried blood. It's Hamlet. It's me.
'Oh, from this time forth,
My thoughts be bloody or be nothing worth.'
Father Mac was going to take that bit out this morning. I stood up for myself, I wouldn't let him. I made a decision last night. So the play, it's taken on a whole new dimension. It'll be my farewell, see? That's how I'll say goodbye. I've owned up, but they don't take any notice. No one except Bowker even believes I was there. I don't care. The readiness is all. Because I've decided something. On my own. If they won't sack me I'll come anyway.

Silence. DOMINIC *goes on working at the wall.*

Is that a gun he's carrying? Dom? I'll come with you.
DOMINIC: No, Tim.
TIM: Well, what else am I going to do? I can't take any more of this place, not now. That is a gun, isn't it?
DOMINIC: We've been through this. Your old man will come after you and drag you back home.
TIM: He'd have to find me first. I'm coming with you.
DOMINIC: This is not a piece of theatre, Tim.
TIM: No? I caught myself this morning in the middle of that speech. I thought, what is this like? You up the ladder, attacking the wall with a brush. That was theatre for you.

33

DOMINIC: Bullshit.

TIM: It was. And it's my play too. I was there. I'm not an attendant lord. [*He stains his clothes with paint.*] I'm in this too. I'm going.

> NORMA *comes in.*

NORMA: I hope you've eaten every last skerrick— [*Seeing the wall*] What kind of mad dog are you? They're going to have to take you out and shoot you. I thought better of you, boy. I thought you had something. But you're just a mug lair. [*She calls out the door, then turns back to* DOMINIC.] Have you got it in for her, or what? Are you trying to make her lose her job?

DOMINIC: The hero's widow? No risk of that. They've got her booked for the Parade. She's going to speak to the troops next Sunday.

> JENNY *comes in, sees the wall.*

JENNY: I see. Norma, would you ring the college, and ask Father Rector to come down here?

NORMA: I'll get the Division Master. He could bring his strap. And I'll stay and watch.

JENNY: No. Father Rector. As soon as possible.

> NORMA *goes.*

[*To* DOMINIC] Get to the bathroom. Clean yourself up. Move.

> *He goes.*

And you, what's your name?

TIM: Donohue, Matron.

JENNY: Get him fresh pyjamas from the hall press.

TIM: We've made a mess. Haven't we?

JENNY: What did you do?

TIM: I helped.

JENNY: Then help him get clean.

> TIM *goes. She looks at the wall then strips the bed.* NORMA *returns.*

NORMA: Well, you did say you wanted the place painted.

JENNY: Another job for your husband.

NORMA: He'll be days in the drill-hall. Working on Connolly's previous effort. Look at this mess. You're copping it sweet. No, it's more than that. You're involved.

JENNY: Father Rector's coming?

NORMA: I left a message.

JENNY: I hope he gets it.

NORMA: He will. Look at you. You've broken Norma's golden rule. You've got involved.

JENNY: Those sheets will need soaking.

TIM *returns. The college bell rings in the distance.*

He can't be clean yet.

TIM: He said he'd manage on his own. Sorry about the mess, Norma, but it had to be done.

NORMA: You only watched, didn't you? Same as always.

TIM: I was in it. Look at me.

NORMA: Well, what is it?

TIM: Can't you tell? A man with a gun.

NORMA: Just a lot of smudges on a wall.

TIM: It's a protest, can't you see?

'How stand I then
That have a father killed, a mother stained,
Excitements of my reason, and my blood,
And let all sleep...'

NORMA: Oh, put a cork in it.

TIM: No. Listen. '...while to my shame I see
The imminent death of twenty thousand men,'

JENNY: Donohue...

TIM: '...That for a fantasy and trick of fame
Go to their graves like beds; fight for a plot
Which is not tomb enough and continent
To hide the slain? O from this time forth,
My thoughts be bloody or be nothing worth.'

D'ARCY *is at the door.*

D'ARCY: Donohue. You're late for lunch.

TIM: Yes, Father.

D'ARCY: You'd better clean up first.

TIM: But Father...

35

D'ARCY: On your way, Donohue.

TIM: Father... Yes, Father.

He goes.

JENNY: I was expecting the Rector.

D'ARCY: I heard. I thought I should come down.

JENNY: Is he coming?

D'ARCY: [*studying the wall*] Acrylic on plaster. It's an awkward medium. It makes revision difficult.

NORMA: Revision? You mean getting it off? I'm telling you this much, Father. My husband won't touch it. Connolly's cost him his day off already. Not to mention my kids' afternoon on the water-slide. He's not doing this wall as well.

JENNY: It's staying here for the Rector to see.

D'ARCY: Norma, fetch a bucket of warm water and a scrubbing brush.

NORMA: I'm not touching it.

D'ARCY: Get me a bucket, and a brush, and some sugar soap, something like that.

He takes off his robe and rolls up his shirt-sleeves.

NORMA: You can't do it, Father. It's not right.

JENNY: No, it's not.

D'ARCY: A bucket, a brush and some soap.

NORMA *goes.*

JENNY: Leave it. It has to be seen.

D'ARCY: Why?

JENNY: It's his answer. You made him an offer this morning, didn't you? He was asked to paint something outside the Hopcroft library. But he went to work on this wall. That's an answer.

D'ARCY: Only while it's visible.

JENNY: What are you scared of, Father? If he goes, what happens to you?

D'ARCY: That's not important. It's his future that matters.

JENNY: So you've got him a prize he doesn't deserve—

D'ARCY: I know why you might feel that. But he does deserve it. And he needs it.

JENNY: But he'll get it only if everybody lies.

D'ARCY: Lies?

JENNY: All right, covers up. That wall. And now this one. But he meant them both to be read. I mean seen. No, read. Like a statement.

NORMA *returns with bucket and brush.*

Sorry, they won't be needed.

NORMA: Make up your minds. This is not even my department.

D'ARCY: Leave them, please. And help Connolly back in here.

NORMA: I'm not joining the rescue committee. He's broken enough rules. He's got to cop the consequences.

JENNY: Exactly. Don't you see he's chosen?

D'ARCY: Impulse. I think he may already regret this.

JENNY: He finished it. That's not regret.

DOMINIC *returns in clean pyjamas.*

NORMA: No, it's just showing off.

She goes.

D'ARCY: Tell me, who was this aimed at?

DOMINIC: I don't know. The Rector. The school. Everyone.

D'ARCY: But did you have them in mind when you began?

JENNY: This took time. He had something in mind!

D'ARCY: Expulsion?

DOMINIC: It happens to plenty of people. They survive.

D'ARCY: Survive, yes. But do they thrive?

DOMINIC: Please. Don't talk about London and Paris.

D'ARCY: It's not wrong for a young artist to want to be surrounded by great art.

JENNY: Don't go for his weakness. Let him stand by what he's done.

D'ARCY: Ambition's not a weakness. He has other weaknesses. Dominic. Don't turn away. Look me in the eye. You like to think of yourself as a subversive. Don't you?

JENNY: Stop this.

D'ARCY: As a subversive. Yes or no?

DOMINIC: Yes.

D'ARCY: Good. The subversive thing, the truly subversive thing, would be to make use of the system in order to challenge it.

JENNY: That's not right.

D'ARCY: It's an old tradition and a fairly honourable one.

JENNY: Fairly honourable.

D'ARCY: This is not the middle ages. Good men don't disappear into caves. Goodness and talent express themselves in action. And effective action involves compromise. Tell me you're willing to clean this off and no more will be heard of it.

JENNY: You can't guarantee that.

D'ARCY: I can do my best. And if he agrees, I promise you a clean wall. [*To* DOMINIC] I won't speak about Europe. Let's follow the other path. Say you are expelled. You'll get a job. What sort of job? Carrying bricks? Digging up the roads? For what sort of money? What sort of equipment will that buy you? Butcher's paper and a carpenter's pencil.

DOMINIC: I can manage like that for a year. Then I'll do my HSC and get to art school.

D'ARCY: And in the meantime? You'll feel such anger about what you've given away. And soon you'll want things. Not things, opportunities. Encouragement. Special consideration. And you'll be asked: 'What have you done? Where have you come from?' And you'll say: 'Well, I could have had, I could have done, I could have been...'

JENNY: Stop this!

D'ARCY: Not yet. The year I was ordained I saw a great film. A man without prospects sat in the back of a taxicab and said: 'I could have had class. I could have been a contender.' Could have had. Could have been. This country is full of people locked into those constructions, the litany of failure. They could have, they should have, they might have. But they fail through lack of talent. Or luck, or opportunity. Don't embrace failure out of wilfulness. Suicidal wilfulness, which is your true weakness. See, it's on this wall. A man with a gun, unable to injure anyone but himself. Am I right? If you're opposed to killing, you should be against suicide. In any form. [*Silence.*] What do you say?

JENNY: I'll go and find the Rector.

D'ARCY: He's in the city until tomorrow afternoon. Dominic? We'll do it, yes?

JENNY: It won't come off.

D'ARCY: It will. With a bit of muscle. [*Scrubbing the wall hard*] See, he's not stopping me. Do you have any sugar soap?

JENNY *goes*. D'ARCY *scrubs*. DOMINIC *watches in silence*.

SCENE TWO

Night. The wall is cleaned and repainted. DOMINIC *is in bed, sketching.* JENNY *enters.*

DOMINIC: This is going to be for you. When it's finished.

JENNY: It's nearly lights out. Have you cleaned your teeth?

DOMINIC: Yes, matron. I have the Colgate ring of confidence.

JENNY: Would you put that away, please? Listen. I have something to tell you. This afternoon, the telephone rang. It was a voice I didn't know. Lady Hopcroft, calling to thank me for something I haven't agreed to do, for speaking at the passing-out parade on Sunday. She said she looked forward to sitting with me, and how sorry she was that Luke hadn't lived to take up his scholarship, what a fine surgeon he would have been, what honour he would have brought to the Hopcroft name. And I ...

Pause.

DOMINIC: What?

JENNY: I told her about the drill-hall. I guessed right, it was news to her. She said she'd known you were a firebrand, that was her word, but not a vandal, also her word. She wasn't pleased to hear she'd been... well, kept in the dark. She'd have to think long and hard about this year's scholarship.

DOMINIC: Think about someone else.

JENNY: Yes. You'll think I've done you some damage—

DOMINIC: Haven't you?

JENNY: I don't think bargains are struck. I think you either live within a system, believing in it, or you take yourself out of it. No halfway measures.

DOMINIC: So I'm out of it. Couldn't you let that be my decision?

JENNY: I'd like to believe it was. It certainly helps me to think better of you.

She picks up his cup, and moves to the door.

DOMINIC: You didn't do this so you could think better of me. You did it because you're angry. Your husband's dead and I'm alive. Lady Hopcroft said, 'Sorry poor old Luke missed the prize', and you dobbed me in.

JENNY: Dobbed you in. I'm not one of your schoolboy mates. I told her the truth.

DOMINIC: The widow's curse.

JENNY: That's enough. It's lights out.

DOMINIC: You've stuffed up my life and it's lights out.

JENNY: Where did you dredge up all this self-pity? On your first night here you were ready to face the world on your own.

DOMINIC: But then I had two days thinking and dreaming about Europe. What I could see, what I could do. How do I let go of that?

JENNY: For God's sake! You can get there on a boat for a few hundred dollars. Go out and earn it like everyone else. The world is nowhere near as frightening as Father D'Arcy painted it. I think you'll survive, maybe even thrive out there. It's quite an interesting place.

She has her hand on the light switch.

DOMINIC: Well, why have you given up on it?

JENNY: Given up on what?

DOMINIC: The world. Why have you come here?

JENNY: To do a job I can do well. To earn my living. That's what you do in the world. Go back to bed. Go to sleep.

DOMINIC: You're here to bury yourself. With him.

JENNY: He's not buried here!

DOMINIC: For you he is. Jenny, you're a young woman...

JENNY: A young woman. If I was the old Matron, you wouldn't care, would you?

DOMINIC: She was dead years before they came for her. You're not. But you'll do what they all do here. You'll die slowly.

JENNY: You think Norma's dead? And Kev?

DOMINIC: They've got a life across the river. A vegie garden, and beer in the fridge, and a rubber tyre hanging over the water for the kids

to swing on. They come here to make a quid. Everyone else...
you'll hear them at the Parade. This island is their world. The
Regiment and the Band and the Team and the Honour Board and...

JENNY: And the Hopcroft scholarship?

Silence.

DOMINIC: Okay. Okay. Okay! You win. Shit. Yes. You win.

JENNY: There's nothing to win.

DOMINIC: Okay. You were right. No bargains. All right?

JENNY: Yes. All right. I think it's for the best.

DOMINIC: Well, I'll find out, won't I?

JENNY: Yes.

DOMINIC: On my own.

JENNY: Yes. Good night. [*She turns the light out.*] I'll make this job
work.

DOMINIC: Sure. But you'll waste yourself. Away, I mean. Waste away.
Waste your life. Isn't it bad enough that his was wasted?

JENNY: What did you say?

DOMINIC: You heard. Bloody wasted. His death was useless. Stupid.

JENNY: He was saving lives. You think you'll ever do anything that
useless?

She turns away.

DOMINIC: I'm sorry. Too far again. Much too far.

*He gets out of bed, puts an arm around her. She does not
pull away.*

JENNY: No. You were right. About burying myself. I think I died with
him. And I was angry. With you. You see, we used to plan our own
time on the Hopcroft. Which hospital and who'd be there to learn
from. And how we'd find a little flat somewhere. We'd be told to
see the Cotswolds and Cornwall and the deer in Epping Forest.
And Portugal and Venice and... We were going to see everything.
The world. We were going in June. And he was killed in April. It
shouldn't have happened.

DOMINIC: That means it was useless.

JENNY: I don't let myself think that.

DOMINIC: Is it all right if I keep holding you?

JENNY: They buried him, what was left of him, in a plastic bag. He used to say he didn't have surgeon's hands. They were big. Clumsy. Too much rowing, he said, spreads the hands. And he'd make them look like plates of meat. He made me laugh. All the time. You can't imagine how much I used to laugh. I'm not like this. My life isn't about death and burial. It's straight-down-the-line suburban. No horror stories. Not even a dog run over. No cruelty, no scars. Three sisters and two brothers and good parents and a nice school, and holidays on the South Coast. And then training at the Mater, and meeting Luke. Who wasn't hero material at all. A man with big hands. Textbook happy ending. And here I am. [*Pause.*] You're very quiet. Even your heart-beat has slowed down. Dear God, you're crying.

DOMINIC: No.

JENNY: Not for me. I'm all right. Look. Is it the happy family stuff? I forgot. You haven't had much of that, have you? Talk to me. Or don't you want to?

DOMINIC: I want to. Have to. My father was on the Burma railway.

JENNY: He died there? No, he can't have.

DOMINIC: Well, maybe he did. But he came back. He hadn't done anything heroic. He survived. But when I was four he died. On the island, on Norfolk. On my mother's family's place, where he was working. He survived the Japs and malnutrition and jungle fever, and he died in a little shed on a farm. And my mother died too. My grandparents woke me up, told me there'd been an accident. We all went to church, and there they were in their boxes, and everybody patted my head and it was all over. My grandfather had the shed torn down. Next year they packed me off to the nuns at Bowral. Nothing was said. I never knew anything but the date. Last Christmas, D'Arcy signed me up for that art workshop. I stayed at the People's Palace. I was free for the first time in my life. Unsupervised, they say here. I did some unsupervised study. I went into the public library and got out the newspaper files. I went straight to the date. He shot her twice through the heart. Then blew the back off his own head. That's what I put on your wall. The inside of his head. Not mine. His. I'm sick of holding it in. Nobody knows I know. Except you.

42

JENNY: I won't tell.

DOMINIC: And I'm scared I'm just a fake. I think I believe what I believe, but then I think, maybe I don't give a stuff about the world. Maybe I only worry about the inside of my head. Or do I mean the inside of his? And hers, when she saw him coming towards her. If she saw him. What did she think?

JENNY: How could you ever know? It might be best to stop thinking about it.

DOMINIC: How do I do that! How the hell do I stop! [*Pause.*] Sorry. [*Silence.*] What are you thinking? Are you thinking I'm mad too? Tainted. That's what my grandparents think. I know. They're scared. They pay the bills and send me a David Jones parcel once a term. Socks and hankies and a tin of IXL jam. Are you scared of me?

JENNY: No.

DOMINIC: Could I... sort of lie down with you?

JENNY: No. Well... halfway.

> *She sits back and holds him.*

DOMINIC: I'd love to...

JENNY: What?

DOMINIC: To see you naked.

JENNY: No.

DOMINIC: Just look at you, see you like that. I drew you like that.

JENNY: Did you now?

DOMINIC: It's a good drawing.

JENNY: Then the reality could only be a disappointment.

DOMINIC: You reckon? Let me be the judge of that.

> *He giggles. She laughs.*

JENNY: No. This is enough. Actually, it's too much. But it's enough. It can't go further.

DOMINIC: Why not?

JENNY: I wouldn't want to limit your imagination.

> *They are laughing.*

DOMINIC: This is amazing. Just being this close.

JENNY: Haven't you ever had a girlfriend?

DOMINIC: Not like this. Not... horizontal.

JENNY: Halfway horizontal.

A twig snaps outside. She rises suddenly.

Are there any animals around here?

DOMINIC: There's a few on the staff.

JENNY: Out there. I heard something moving. [*She looks out into the night.*] Nothing. It's time you were asleep.

DOMINIC: Stay here with me.

JENNY: I couldn't. Into bed.

DOMINIC: Please stay.

JENNY: That would be taking us out into deep water.

DOMINIC: Well?

JENNY: I have a life to make here. I'd rather remember you as a patient. Good night, Dominic.

She hurries out of the room.

SCENE THREE

Bright daylight. D'ARCY *enters via the verandah door.* DOMINIC'*s bed is empty.* JENNY *enters with a vase of flowers.*

JENNY: I didn't hear you come in.

D'ARCY: They're very pretty.

JENNY: Yes.

D'ARCY: An unusual gesture.

JENNY: There's a garden full of them. It's in a terrible state. I spent this morning pruning.

D'ARCY: You're making the place your own.

JENNY: I'd like to change the pictures. There's an awful lot of battles. St Ignatius wounded at... wherever it is... St James Northcott on a stretcher beside a cannon. And as for St Michael turning Lucifer out of heaven...

D'ARCY: Tiepolo. It's a very fine picture.

JENNY: Not for a dispensary. I'm hoping Connolly might draw these before he leaves.

D'ARCY: He's not going quite yet. Is he?

JENNY: He is leaving the infirmary. Doctor Lenane will be here tomorrow at lunchtime. Then if all is well, the stitches come out, and he's a free man.

D'ARCY: A free man. Mm. Where is he?

JENNY: I let him go down to the river. He's quite mobile, and he's got a stick to keep him off the leg. I thought some fresh air would do him good.

D'ARCY: You don't have to explain. This is your domain down here. He may be out on the water. He keeps an old dinghy hidden in a little cove. Normally he's careful to take it out only after dark. On a night without a moon I sometimes see the light of a cigarette out on the river.

> JENNY *is going.*

What did you mean, a free man?

JENNY: He'll be up and about.

D'ARCY: You meant more than that. You were smiling to yourself. Have you ever met Lady Hopcroft?

JENNY: Not face to face.

D'ARCY: Not face to face. She's rather angry. Somebody told her about the drill-hall.

JENNY: Yes. I told her.

D'ARCY: I guessed right. I thought it must have been you. How could you do such a thing?

JENNY: You think I've interfered?

D'ARCY: Yes, I do.

JENNY: The first time we met, not even a week ago, you tried to enlist me in a cause.

D'ARCY: Which you refused. And now you've said something which could do this boy enormous damage.

JENNY: Does he deserve the prize? My husband fitted the bill. This boy doesn't.

D'ARCY: I see. Your husband didn't get to enjoy the scholarship, so this boy shouldn't.

JENNY: [*loudly, over him*] No! But if somebody has chosen a path of questioning and rebellion, should he go the way of someone like

Luke? That's the question. Is it fair? And is it right for him?

D'ARCY: I don't see how you'd know on one week's acquaintance.

JENNY: And do you know even after six years? Do you really see him? How close to the edge he's living? I think you see what you choose to see.

D'ARCY: You can't know how offensive that is.

JENNY: And you say what you choose to say. Lady Hopcroft is not the only one who's been deceived, Father. Dangerous D'Arcy, you said they called you. A red-hot radical.

D'ARCY: I think the word was liberal.

JENNY: Forget the words. You implied you were powerless. Ignored. That's not true.

D'ARCY: I had Lady Hopcroft's ear. That's all. Now she won't return my telephone calls, thanks to you.

JENNY: I told her the truth.

D'ARCY: Tell me the truth, Matron. Do you think you'll take this much trouble over all your patients?

> BOWKER *is on the verandah, in his blazer, carrying a pile of schoolbooks.*

Ah, Mr Bowker. Well done. [*To* JENNY] I thought it was time he started some serious study for the HSC.

JENNY: The HSC?

D'ARCY: We live in hope, Matron. A pity to leave him unprepared. [*Searching*] I don't see his Art History...

BOWKER: They're all there.

> D'ARCY *finds an envelope between two books.*

What's this?

BOWKER: Nothing.

D'ARCY: An empty envelope?

BOWKER: There's just something of Connolly's...

D'ARCY: Something? You mean a drawing?

BOWKER: It's sort of... private.

> D'ARCY *opens the envelope, finds the nude drawing.* JENNY *sees it.*

D'ARCY: Very fine.

JENNY: It's time Connolly came in.

She hurries out to the river as BOWKER *puts away the drawing.*

D'ARCY: There's no need to be embarrassed about a nude, you know.

BOWKER: No, Father.

D'ARCY: It's a new direction for Connolly.

BOWKER: Yes, Father.

D'ARCY: Kind of you to deliver these.

BOWKER: I'd... I'd like to stay and see Connolly.

D'ARCY: I'd rather you didn't. I need to see him myself. All in order for play night?

BOWKER: Yes, Father. My mother's got it under control, the programmes and supper and the official party. She's a brilliant organiser.

D'ARCY: A remarkable woman. Great energy and great taste. You're a lucky man.

BOWKER: I know. She and I have been talking. Trying to sort out my future.

D'ARCY: I thought that was already decided.

BOWKER: Well, not since she had a call from Lady Hopcroft.

D'ARCY: Lady Hopcroft.

BOWKER: They're good mates. She's Mum's godmother, actually. She... she dropped a few hints about the scholarship.

D'ARCY: When was this?

BOWKER: Last night, I think. Here was I thinking it'd have to be Fitzgerald. He's the one with the brains. But she seemed to say they might be considering me.

D'ARCY: But you're headed for the military college.

BOWKER: Well, I've been a bit iffy about it since... since last weekend and the dinner and everything, wondering why I was doing it.

D'ARCY: You've got every reason to do it.

BOWKER: Well, now I'm not so sure. Anyway, Mum's seeing the Rector this afternoon. He sent for her just now.

D'ARCY: Well, my congratulations. If that's the way things are to go.

BOWKER: Did you think it'd be Fitzgerald too?

D'ARCY: Bowker, not a word to Connolly about this. Not a word to anyone. Think if this news got back to Fitzgerald before the proper time. It might damage his performance in the HSC. And we wouldn't want that, would we?

He hurries out into the hall as DOMINIC *follows* JENNY *in from outside. He has his stick, and a sketch-pad under his arm.*

JENNY: Where's Father D'Arcy? He wanted to see Connolly.
BOWKER: Gone up to College. I think I might have upset him.
JENNY: Where's that drawing?

BOWKER *gives it to her. She hands it to* DOMINIC.

Please destroy it.

She goes.

DOMINIC: What is it? [*Opening it*] Oh.
BOWKER: You won't tear it up, will you?
DOMINIC: I thought you'd done that already.
BOWKER: No way. I showed it to Mum.

DOMINIC *opens his pad and continues drawing.*

She's here doing supper for the play. Pity you'll miss it. Donohue's Hamlet, I mean, not the supper. That's good. Really good. The river.
DOMINIC: It's not finished. There'll be a boat.
BOWKER: Can you really draw and talk at the same time?
DOMINIC: I'd rather just draw.
BOWKER: Will you at least listen?

DOMINIC *nods.*

I felt pretty stupid walking back from here the other night. I didn't go to bed. I went down by the river. I found that dinghy of yours. Yes, I've always known where you keep it. I went out on the water. It was amazing. So dark and still. Just the oars dipping the water. You know what I thought? All these years I should have been a rower.
DOMINIC: Then you wouldn't have been Captain of the First Eleven.
BOWKER: Don't keep taking the piss. I'm trying to tell you something.
DOMINIC: That you wish you'd been a rower?
BOWKER: That I wish a few other things had been different. I'm not going to Duntroon.

DOMINIC: Oh.

BOWKER: I'm going to uni. Economics-law. Then maybe business school overseas, maybe Harvard. But anyway, not the army. That's certain. I'll live at home. And that's what Mum wants to talk to you about. She wants you to stay with us. Next year. She'd like to... take you under her wing. She knows so many people...

DOMINIC: Like your father's mates?

BOWKER: Not just politicians. Artistic people. All the big painters come to the house. Do you want to know a secret? My mother's against the war now. She's been asked to join a committee with some artists. But she can't really compromise my Dad.

DOMINIC: Of course not.

BOWKER: Go easy. She's impressed by what you did. She wanted to see the wall of the drill-hall. And I showed her this. She was knocked out. I didn't tell her who the woman is. She just took it as... a piece of art. Out of your head.

DOMINIC: It was.

BOWKER: Well, of course. Lucky she didn't ask me what I thought. It gave me a horn. Sorry. But it's true. Anyway, Mum thinks it's great. A great advance.

DOMINIC: Brian, I've been a shit to you all year. Why do you want this? Why would you even want to be friends with me?

BOWKER: Because you're bloody brilliant. Look at this blazer, all the lines on the pocket. You could have had twice what I've got, with half the effort. And you passed it up for your beliefs. You went solo. I don't go with what you believe, but I admire your guts. I'd like us to be friends. I'd like to be able to say in the year two thousand, 'Dominic Connolly? Yes, I was at school with him. We were mates'. We have been, haven't we? We could be still. We should be. My Dad's ready to shake hands. My mother's ready to show you the world.

DOMINIC: If I stay.

BOWKER: Yes. And they'll make it all right for you. [*Silence.*] Don't be bloody mad! Do your exams and give the Rector his mural. You owe it to yourself.

DOMINIC: No, I don't.

BOWKER: All right. You owe it to the College. You couldn't be sitting here drawing that river and that boat, if it wasn't for this place and the J's. You wouldn't even know how to argue if it wasn't for them. They gave you all the words you need.

DOMINIC: All the words? There's so many they wouldn't even know.

BOWKER: They must know something. Seventy places a year, and a waiting-list of three hundred.

DOMINIC: Three hundred little boys lining up for the punt. And only the lucky seventy get shunted across—

BOWKER: We are lucky.

DOMINIC: —for six years on the island. It's a long stretch. But you end up a College Man, in a royal blue blazer, with your life written on the pocket.

BOWKER: You know I don't think this pocket is important.

DOMINIC: Then why are you wearing it in the middle of the day?

BOWKER: Official duties. For your friend's play night. Look, you could have had twice this and more. How many times do I have to say it? You're brilliant. My mother and father think so. And they're offering you a home. They think you've got a real future.

DOMINIC: What if I haven't? What if there's no future?

BOWKER: It's a pretty low-risk investment.

DOMINIC: Say they make it all right for me. And then I never achieve anything? Or hit the piss? Or get called up and don't go? They'll have blown their investment.

BOWKER: All right, I can't use words like you...

DOMINIC: I don't want to be an investment.

BOWKER: What do you want? Nobody can work it out.

DOMINIC: I dunno. To be able to fail. To get things wrong. To be loved whatever happens.

BOWKER: You would be.

DOMINIC: The way you are? Your father pats you on the back every time you add a line to that pocket. Your mother wishes you were me. You call that love?

BOWKER: At least my father didn't take a shotgun to my mother in the middle of the night.

> DOMINIC *attacks* BOWKER *suddenly, bringing him to the ground, raising a fist to smash his face.*

50

Dominic, don't!

DOMINIC *stops, dazed, panting.*

DOMINIC: How did you know?

BOWKER: Oh, Christ. Christmas Day at Palm Beach. You had that fight with my Dad. You said he worked for a government of killers, remember? Then you pissed off down the beach. I went and found your journal, looked through it. I saw the little drawings. That old shed. I've sat on that all this year. It's stopped me from thumping you a couple of times. I'm really really sorry.

DOMINIC: Sorry it happened? Or sorry you read it?

BOWKER: Both, of course.

DOMINIC: I could have killed you just then. Smashed your face in, and kept going.

BOWKER: Yes, you could.

DOMINIC: And you're very strong. Shit. I go too far.

BOWKER: Yes. Too far. Promise me one thing. When you see me, years from now, come up to me. Don't run away. Don't be shut off. Because I will be. I know more about myself than you think.

Abruptly BOWKER *envelops* DOMINIC *in a clumsy but powerful embrace. Just as abruptly he lets go and hurries out, leaving* DOMINIC *alone in the middle of the room.*

SCENE FOUR

Late afternoon. Sounds of rowers on the river. On a spare bed, a pile of school khakis. JENNY *is removing stitches from* DOMINIC's *thigh.*

DOMINIC: It tickles.

JENNY: You're going to have quite a scar. It'll be a talking point in years to come. There. A free man.

DOMINIC: I've got something to give you before I go. My drawing. It's the Vikings on the river.

JENNY: I'm not sure I want them.

DOMINIC: You can decide tomorrow morning. I'll bring it down before I go. Before the Parade. You haven't told me. Are you going to be there with them?

JENNY: You can see yourself out. I've got a couple of boys waiting for sick parade.

She goes out of the room. DOMINIC *changes into his uniform as* TIM *comes in from the verandah.*

TIM: Well, I got through it. I wish you'd been there. They sat up and took notice.

DOMINIC: You were good?

TIM: The readiness is all. Actually, I came down the other night to show you a bit of it.

DOMINIC: When?

TIM: After the dress rehearsal. I was all fired up. I was planning to stand in the doorway and surprise you. But... you were with her.

DOMINIC: I remember. She heard a sound.

TIM: She got up and looked out. And I ran.

DOMINIC: You didn't mention it to anyone?

TIM shakes his head.

You're sure? You could get her into trouble if people misunderstood.

TIM: Misunderstood?

DOMINIC: Nothing happened.

TIM: That wasn't nothing. Did it happen often?

DOMINIC: That night only. The next day it was like I'd dreamt it.

TIM: Some dream. Anyway, you missed a private performance.

DOMINIC: I'll see you act again.

TIM: You reckon? You're going, aren't you? Well, aren't you?

DOMINIC: Tomorrow morning, first thing. While they're all getting ready for the Parade. I think they're scared I might stage some demo. So they'll frog-march me to the punt, and Brother Doolan will drive me to the train.

TIM: And after that?

DOMINIC: Dunno. There's a plane ticket to Norfolk Island waiting at the airport, but I somehow don't think I'll ever get there.

TIM: Have you got money?

DOMINIC: Ten bucks.

TIM: I've got about fifty in cash and more in a bank account.

DOMINIC: I couldn't take your money, Tim.

TIM: But if I came with you...

DOMINIC: No, Tim. You'd get us both into strife.

TIM: I asked. I'm sixteen, they can't touch you. I can't get a license yet, or vote, or join the army, but I can't be dragged back to Goulburn, or back here. Look, I'm hopeless at everything, a total dud at every sport, a joke in the cadets, a slug in class. I only come alive in the play, and that's once a year. Being your friend made this place... [*He wants to say 'bearable'.*] I can't face it without you.

DOMINIC: And I can't take this on, mate.

TIM: Have you had a better friend than me this year? Everyone else dropped you. I know I give you the shits, but that's mainly this place. I can be very strong and independent. You'll see.

DOMINIC: Do you know what it'd be like?

TIM: Do you? Have you ever survived on your own? Even staying at the People's Palace that time, you had that course to go to, and all those art people. Tomorrow night there'll be nobody. Listen to me. I'll bring my bank-book and my transistor. And I won't be a sook. Fucking well take me!

　　　Pause.

DOMINIC: Oh, what the hell. Okay, get an exeat next Sunday and I'll meet you at Central.

TIM: No. I'm going with you.

DOMINIC: How? They're taking me to the train. They wouldn't even let you on the punt.

TIM: We'll go tonight. It's nearly dark.

DOMINIC: Yes, but—

TIM: And you can't go back to College, even for the night. Imagine sleeping in dorm, knowing you could be... out there. And what if Dangerous gets hold of you? He'll have you starting on that mural.

DOMINIC: No way.

TIM: That's what you say now. Don't risk it. See? Strong and independent.

DOMINIC: Okay. Okay, here's the plan. I've got one thing to do here...

TIM: Yeah, you've got to say goodbye to your girlfriend.

DOMINIC: I've got to give the Matron her present, dickhead. You find some civvies, or we'll look like Bib and Bub getting on the train. Here's my locker-key. Get into my locker. My cigarettes are in my left footie boot. And there's ten bucks in the back of *Riders In The Chariot*. Soon as she's finished sick parade, I'll meet you at the dinghy.

FATHER D'ARCY *is at the hall door.*

D'ARCY: Out of the bondage of the sickbed. I enjoyed your play, Donohue.

TIM: Thank you, Father.

D'ARCY: You missed a fine performance, Connolly.

DOMINIC: I could have had a private preview down here.

TIM *giggles.*

D'ARCY: Good to see you graduating to male roles. What has Father Mac got for you next year? Brutus? Richard the Second? Or something modern?

TIM: Oh, the sky's the limit, Father.

D'ARCY: That's the stuff. Off you go, now.

DOMINIC: See you at roll-call.

TIM: Yes.

He goes.

D'ARCY: A happy man. It doesn't take much. Just the fulfilment of our aspirations. They'll probably give the Hopcroft to Mr Bowker. [*Pause.*] Rather a waste, don't you think?

DOMINIC: It'll be great for him. He wants to go to the Harvard Business School.

D'ARCY: That sounds insincere.

DOMINIC: It's not. I've got to see the Matron before I go.

D'ARCY: Yes. Father Rector told us your news in the common-room. Brother Doolan is putting you on the train in the morning. They seem to want you off the premises before the passing-out parade. And I thought 'dangerous' was my nickname.

DOMINIC: Well. I'll see you up at College. [*He takes the drawing and goes towards the hall door.*] Excuse me.

D'ARCY: A drawing for Matron? Her? The other one was impressive.

I could sense real engagement.

DOMINIC: This one isn't of her. It's just for her.

D'ARCY: I have something for her too. You could deliver it.

DOMINIC: What is it?

D'ARCY: A speech. She'll be on the dais tomorrow. At the Parade.

DOMINIC: Will she?

D'ARCY: Oh, yes.

DOMINIC: She's said so?

D'ARCY: According to Father Rector. We thought she might need a little help. Perhaps you could hear it through for me? See how it sounds?

DOMINIC: I'm in a bit of a hurry.

D'ARCY: It won't take a minute. Let me try it out. I've spent hours on it. It's the last thing I'll ever ask of you.

Pause. DOMINIC *looks out towards the riverbank.*

Please.

DOMINIC *nods, sits on the end of a bed.*

'I am not a soldier. That's to say, I'm not a member of the regiment you see before you today. But I want to pay tribute to someone, who though not himself a soldier, died in the name of our country. Our Patron Saint called himself Christ's Corporal. He exchanged his sword and shield for the insignia of the Society of Jesus; but he died for his beliefs, died at the hands of enemies of those beliefs, and so he died a soldier's death. The man we honour today died also for his beliefs. But they were not merely his...'

DOMINIC *rises abruptly.*

DOMINIC: Father—

D'ARCY: 'It might be said that the death of Dr Luke Walsh was of no use to any cause. But I believe that such a death is not useless, for...'

DOMINIC: I have to go.

He heads towards the door. Outside, the light is going.

D'ARCY: Wait. Would you do it? For her?

DOMINIC: What?

D'ARCY: The speech. Give it for her?

DOMINIC: Why!

D'ARCY: You have strong feelings for her. You could say things she might find difficult. And you're a trained public speaker.

DOMINIC: I won't even be here.

D'ARCY: You could change your mind. It's carefully phrased. There's nothing that would do violence to your own beliefs. It doesn't support the war. It simply speaks for her.

DOMINIC: You think so?

D'ARCY: Of course.

DOMINIC: And she'd like to hear it in my mouth?

D'ARCY: I'm sure. Like some others. Lady Hopcroft for one. She'll be there on the dais.

DOMINIC: Oh.

D'ARCY: She's meeting the Rector after the Parade. Nothing's decided yet.

DOMINIC: You said the scholarship was Bowker's.

D'ARCY: Probably, I said.

DOMINIC: He's the right man for it.

D'ARCY: No. He doesn't need the world. You do.

DOMINIC: She knows who I am and what I've done.

D'ARCY: But I've told her you'll speak tomorrow.

Silence.

DOMINIC: You told her that.

D'ARCY: It was the only way I could hold off a decision. Whatever you think, whatever Matron Walsh thinks, I'm not hungry for power. I've never had this amount of influence before. I'll never have it again. All this was for you. And it was only because I took your portfolio down to the city six months ago...

DOMINIC: Portfolio. That's what they call a bunch of shares, isn't it? On the stock-market.

D'ARCY: Don't. Don't twist words. This has all been to give you freedom.

DOMINIC: You spoke for me.

D'ARCY: In your interests.

DOMINIC: You think for me. You thought I'd jump when I heard it was Bowker. And that I'd say these things. And that she'd want to hear them. And it would all work out.

56

D'ARCY: It could.

> DOMINIC *shakes his head.* D'ARCY *paces. He is at the verandah doors.* NORMA *opens the door and comes in with an envelope. She does not see* D'ARCY *at first.*

NORMA: You're a free man, Rembrandt. Well, sign this and you are.

> *She takes out a drawing.*

DOMINIC: Sign what?

NORMA: Your masterpiece. Wedded bliss in the bathtub. Kev found it. I thought he'd hit the roof, but he was flattered. He feels you've captured his inner essence. So he's prepared let bygones be bygones. But he wants your name on it.

D'ARCY: On what?

> NORMA *is surprised, even embarrassed.*

What? Show me.

> NORMA *is reluctant.* DOMINIC *takes the picture from her. After a beat, he shows it to* D'ARCY. *As he stares at it,* JENNY *enters.*

D'ARCY: You think this is freedom?

DOMINIC: Yes.

D'ARCY: This is your final word?

> DOMINIC *nods.*

I warned you. If you go, I discard you.

DOMINIC: No. You said if I go, I cut myself off. Goodbye.

> D'ARCY *turns and goes.*

NORMA: He'll get over it. Soon as he spots some other Rembrandt coming up through the ranks.

> JENNY *picks up the discarded drawing, looks at it, and starts to laugh.*

It's good, isn't it? Not drawn from life, of course. That'd make it dirty. This way, it's art. [*To* DOMINIC] Now, put your name on it for Kev.

> *He does.*

No, not initials, the full thing.

> DOMINIC *signs it and hands it back.*

DOMINIC: There you go.

NORMA: Ta. Now hurry up and get famous. Then we can sell it and have a holiday at Surfers. [*Meaning goodbye, not hurrah*] Hooray.

She goes.

JENNY: What's Donohue doing out there? He's skulking down by the willows.

DOMINIC: Oh, God. I have to go.

JENNY: Is that a bundle he's got?

DOMINIC: Take this. It's for you. Goodbye.

JENNY: You were coming tomorrow morning to say that. Are you leaving now? You can't. I mean, not with him.

DOMINIC: I'll look after him.

JENNY: He has parents. And a career here.

DOMINIC: He's not happy here.

JENNY: But safer.

DOMINIC: He wants to go.

JENNY: He wants to go with you.

DOMINIC: I don't know what you mean.

JENNY: Oh, you do. You don't want blood on your hands. A man like you.

DOMINIC: I'm scared.

JENNY: Of what?

DOMINIC: Of going alone.

A bell rings up at the school.

JENNY: That's what you've chosen. Find out what it's like.

DOMINIC: I don't think I can.

JENNY: You must.

DOMINIC: Must I?

TIM *is in the doorway with a bundle.*

TIM: Come on, I've got it. Cigarettes. Clothes. Money.

He sees JENNY.

DOMINIC: Matches?

TIM: What?

DOMINIC: Matches.

Frightened, TIM *shakes his head slowly.*

Matron, could you please lend me some?

She goes.

TIM: You've told her?

DOMINIC: She worked it out.

TIM: Let's go, quick!

DOMINIC: I can't take you, Tim.

TIM: She said something, didn't she? About me?

DOMINIC: About me. About going it alone. She's right. It's got to be solo, just for now.

TIM: No!

DOMINIC: I'm not what you need.

TIM: You are! [*Silence.*] You mean, I'm not what you need.

DOMINIC: Yes. I'm sorry.

TIM: Making up my mind. I loved that. That was probably the best part.

> JENNY *returns with the matches.* DOMINIC *indicates the bundle.*

DOMINIC: Put that in the dinghy for me?

> TIM *goes.* DOMINIC *picks up the river drawing.*

There's your present.

JENNY: Norma got her husband in the bath. I get a Viking funeral.

DOMINIC: Yes. They let go of their dead.

JENNY: Clunk.

DOMINIC: What?

JENNY: Aren't you supposed to leave the symbolism for the viewer to discover?

DOMINIC: [*putting it on the bed*] Well, I'm young and crude.

> *He goes. She finishes stripping the bed, then picks up the drawing, staring at it.* TIM *appears at the verandah doors.*

JENNY: They've rung the first bell. Don't be late for tea.

TIM: I couldn't see him for more than a few yards. It was too dark on the river. He called something from the other side. I couldn't hear. Where will he go?

JENNY: You'll miss roll-call.

TIM: I don't care. Can I come down and talk to you sometimes? I'm here for another year.

JENNY: If you're sick, I'm at your service.

TIM: Yes. Good night, Matron. [*He goes slowly out across the verandah, then runs back in.*] It's the boat. He's set fire to it. He's pushed it back this way. That's for me. He's done that for me.

The bell rings again.

JENNY: You're late, Donohue.

He goes. The glow of the fire is reflected now in the room. She looks out the windows at the boat burning on the water.

THE END

www.ingramcontent.com/pod-product-compliance
Lightning Source LLC
Chambersburg PA
CBHW041933090426

42744CB00017B/2040